Madhuri in the silent film *Matrubhoomi* (1932)

FROM DARKNESS INTO LIGHT

Perspectives on Film Preservation and Restoration

Edited by Rajesh Devraj

FILM HERITAGE

FOUNDATION

Cover: Nigar Sultana in *Magroor* (1950), 120 mm negative
Back cover and Half-title page: *Chitralekha* (1964), film strip **Courtesy:** Vikram Sharma

ISBN: 978-93-5212-008-6

Designed by Anoop Patnaik for Design Stack.

First published in 2015 by Film Heritage Foundation
Flat No. 707, Floor - 7th, Arun Chambers,
Pandit Madan Mohan Malviya Marg, Tardeo Road,
Mumbai, Maharashtra, India.

Printed and bound in India by Pragati Offset, Hyderabad

THIS BOOK IS DEDICATED TO
ALL THE ARCHIVISTS AND
RESTORERS WHO ARE STRIVING
TO PRESERVE OUR FILM LEGACY
FOR FUTURE GENERATIONS.

Stills from *Sikander* (1941) **Courtesy:** Shiraz Ali

CONTENTS

Shanta Apte in *Kunku* (1937) **Courtesy**: Damle family

FOREWORD

SHIVENDRA SINGH DUNGARPUR, FILM HERITAGE FOUNDATION

In India, cinema is largely perceived as a commercial industry churning out entertainment for the masses. Its value as a visual document of the times is not recognised, nor is it considered an integral part of the nation's heritage, or an art form worthy of preservation. As a result, much of our moving image legacy has been lost, and alarmingly, more continues to be lost every day.

This book is perhaps the first Indian publication dedicated to the topic of film preservation and restoration. Its aim is to draw attention to the deplorable state of our cinematic heritage, and to assess what can be done to rescue this patrimony from extinction. We hope to communicate the urgency of the situation to the film industry, the government and our cinema-loving nation to come forward and act before it is too late.

Aimed primarily at Indian readers, the book provides an introduction to the field of film preservation and restoration, bringing together essays by some of the world's leading experts and archivists. Our 'Global Views' section opens with a piece by filmmaker and cinephile Martin Scorsese, who speaks passionately for the cause of cinema as an art to be preserved for future generations. Articles by Paolo Cherchi Usai (Senior Curator, George Eastman House) and David Walsh (Head of the Digital Collections, Imperial War Museum) discuss current approaches to the conservation of moving images and the impact of digital technology, while Peter Bagrov of Gosfilmofond, the Russian state film archive, provides a film historian's perspective on film restoration.

'Film Preservation Around the World' covers the innovative ways in which international film archives have advanced the cause of film preservation. The article written by Robin Baker, Head Curator, BFI National Archive, is a case study in fund-raising, building awareness of restoration and the marketing of restored classics, while Maciej Molewski 's piece on the KinoRP Project provides an instance of a successful public-private partnership that rescued Poland's cinematic heritage from decades of neglect. There are also pieces from Wenchi Lin of the Taiwan Film Institute and Chalida Uabumrugjit of the Thai Film Archive, both from countries that have had to contend with many of the same issues faced in India, like apathy and lack of funding. The Taiwan Film Institute is an example we in India can learn much from: its ingenious strategies to raise funds and create awareness are truly an inspiration.

We move on to talk about film preservation in India, looking at what has been done so far, and what remains to be done in the future. 'Indian Beginnings' opens with P.K. Nair's anecdotal account of the work done by the National Film Archive of India in building up its film collection, and continues with my own essay on the magic of celluloid, its contemporary relevance and the steps that need to be taken to preserve it for posterity. Three case studies are provided to introduce Indian readers to the work that goes into restoring a film, through examples from our own cinematic heritage: *Kalpana* and *Titas Ekti Nadir Naam*, presented by Cecilia Cenciarelli; and the restoration of Satyajit Ray's Apu Trilogy, described by Lee Kline and Ryan Hullings. Importantly, these studies emphasise that one needs to go beyond the aesthetics of the image, to ensure authenticity, reversibility and transparency in the restoration process. The Indian section closes with the Film Heritage 60, a report on important Indian films which are in urgent need of restoration. Based on research conducted by the Film Heritage Foundation, it provides a detailed inventory of the available material for each film and its current condition, taking stock of our endangered film heritage.

We would like to thank all the contributors who took time out from their busy schedules to write essays, or gave us permission to present their work here: Martin Scorsese, Paolo Cherchi Usai, David Walsh, Peter Bagrov, Robin Baker, Maciej Molewski, Wenchi Lin, Chalida Uabumrungjit, Cecilia Cenciarelli, Lee Kline, Ryan Hullings and P.K. Nair. Special thanks to Rajesh Devraj for conceptualising and editing the book; and to Anoop Patnaik for the book design.

IT IS A BEAUTIFUL AND TRAGIC PARADOX
THAT THE ART OF FILM, WHICH CAPTURES THE
MOVEMENT AND THE FLOW OF LIFE, HAS HAD
TO GRAPPLE WITH ITS MATERIAL MORTALITY
MORE THAN ANY OTHER ARTISTIC MEDIUM.

ANDRE HABIB
Thinking in the Ruins: Around the Films of Bill Morrison

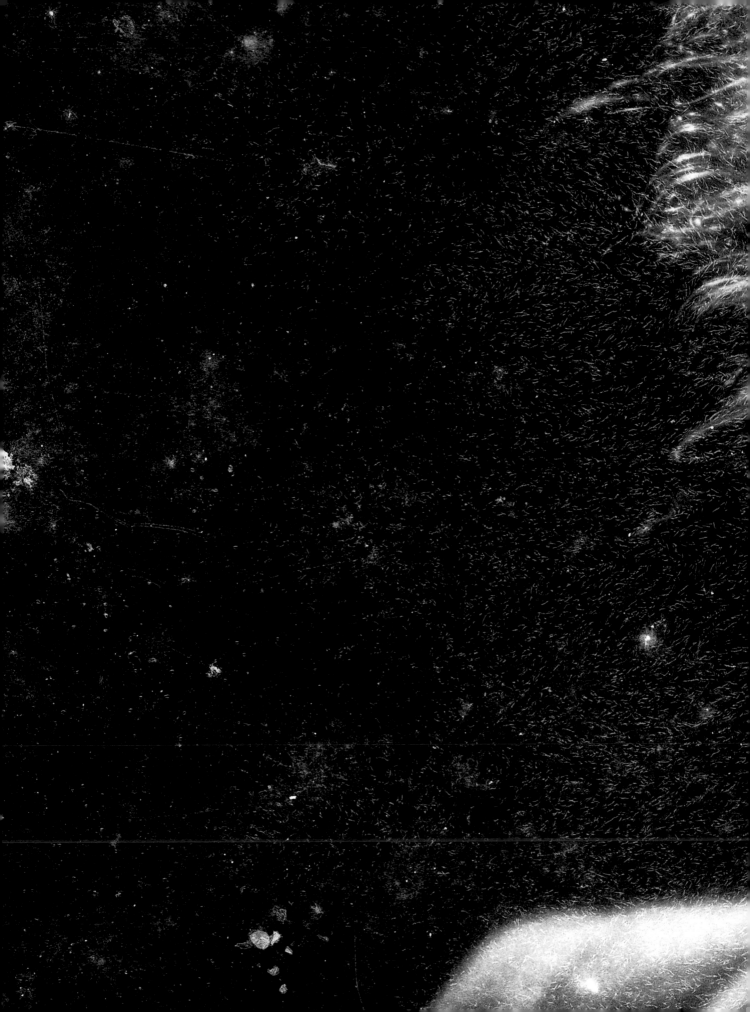

GLOBAL VIEWS

THE PERSISTING VISION:
READING THE LANGUAGE OF CINEMA
MARTIN SCORSESE

Robert Donat in *The Magic Box* (1951) **Image**: Everett Collection

In the film *The Magic Box*, which was made in England in 1950, the great English actor Robert Donat plays William Friese-Greene— one of the people who invented movies. *The Magic Box* was packed with guest stars. It was made for an event called the Festival of Britain. You had about fifty or sixty of the biggest actors in England at the time, all doing for the most part little cameos, including the man who played the policeman—that was Sir Laurence Olivier.

I saw this picture for the first time with my father. I was eight years old. I've never really gotten over the impact that it had. I believe this is what ignited in me the wonder of cinema, and the obsession—with watching movies, making them, inventing them.

Friese-Greene gives everything of himself to the movies, and he dies a pauper. If you know the full story of his life and its end, the line in the film about the invention of the movies—"You must be a very happy man, Mr. Friese-Greene"—of course is ironic, but in some ways it's also true because he's followed his obsession all the way. So it's both disturbing and inspiring. I was very young. I didn't put this into words at the time, but I sensed these things and I saw them up there on the screen.

My parents had a good reason for taking me to the movies all the time, because I had been sick with asthma since I was three years old and I apparently couldn't do any sports, or that's what they told me. But my mother and father did love the movies. They weren't in the habit of reading—that didn't really exist where I came from—and so we connected through the movies.

And I realise now that the warmth of that connection with my family and with the images on the screen gave me something very precious. We were experiencing something fundamental together. We were living through the emotional truths on the screen, often in coded form, which these films from the 1940s and 1950s sometimes expressed in small things: gestures, glances, reactions between the characters, light, shadow. These were things that we normally couldn't discuss or wouldn't discuss or even acknowledge in our lives.

And that's actually part of the wonder. Whenever I hear people dismiss movies as "fantasy" and make a hard distinction between film and life, I think to myself that it's just a way of avoiding the power of cinema. Of course it's not life—it's the invocation of life, it's in an ongoing dialogue with life.

———————————

Frank Capra said, "Film is a disease." I caught the disease early on. I felt it whenever I walked up to the ticket booth with my mother or my father or my brother. You'd go through the doors, up the thick carpet, past the popcorn stand that had that wonderful smell—then to the ticket taker, and then in some of the old theatres there would be another set of doors with little windows and you'd get a glimpse of something magical happening up there on the screen, something special. And as we entered, for me it was like entering a sacred space, a kind of sanctuary where the living world around me seemed to be recreated and played out.

What was it about cinema? What was so special about it? I think I've discovered some of my own answers to that question a little bit at a time over the years.

First of all, there's light.

Light is at the beginning of cinema, of course. It's fundamental—because cinema is created with light, and it's still best seen projected in dark rooms, where it's the only source of light. But light is also at the beginning of everything. Most creation myths start with darkness, and then the real beginning comes with light—which means the creation of forms. Which leads to distinguishing one thing from another, and ourselves from the rest of the world. Recognising patterns, similarities, differences, naming things—interpreting the world. Metaphors—seeing one thing 'in light of' something else. Becoming 'enlightened.' Light is at the core of who we are and how we understand ourselves.

And then, there's movement…

I remember when I was about five or six, someone projected a 16 mm cartoon, and I was allowed to look inside the projector. I saw these little still images passing mechanically through the gate at a very steady rate of speed. In the gate, they were upside down, but they were moving, and on the screen they came out right side up, moving. At least there was the sensation of movement. But it was more than that. Something clicked, right then

and there. "Pieces of time"—that's how James Stewart defined movies in a conversation with Peter Bogdanovich. That wonder I felt when I saw these little figures move—that's what Laurence Olivier feels when he watches those first moving images in that scene from *The Magic Box*.

The desire to make images move, the need to capture movement, seemed to be with us 30,000 years ago in the cave paintings at Chauvet—in one image a bison appears to have multiple sets of legs, and perhaps that was the artist's way of creating the impression of movement. I think this need to recreate movement is a mystical urge. It's an attempt to capture the mystery of who and what we are, and then to contemplate that mystery.

Which brings us to the film of boxing cats that Thomas Edison recorded with his Kinetograph in his Black Maria studio in New Jersey in 1894. Edison, of course, was one of the people who invented film. There's been a lot of debate about who really invented film—there was Edison, the Lumière brothers in France, Friese-Greene and R.W. Paul in England. And actually, you can go back to a man named Louis Le Prince who shot a little home movie in 1888.

And then you could go back even further to the motion studies of Eadweard Muybridge, which were made in the 1870s and 1880s. He would set a number of still cameras side by side and then he'd trigger them to take photos in succession, of people and animals in motion. His employer Leland Stanford challenged him to show that all four of a horse's hooves leave the ground when the horse is running. Muybridge proved they did.

———————————

Does cinema really begin with Muybridge? Should we go all the way back to the cave paintings? In his novel *Joseph and His Brothers*, Thomas Mann writes:

> The deeper we sound, the further down into the lower world of the past we probe and press, the more do we find that the earliest foundations of humanity, its history and culture, reveal themselves unfathomable.

All beginnings are unfathomable—the beginning of human history, the beginning of cinema.

A film by the Lumière brothers of a train arriving at a station in France is commonly recognised as the first publicly projected film. It was shot in 1895. When you watch it, it really is 1895. The way they dress and the way they move—it's now and it's then, at the same time. And that's the third aspect of cinema that makes it so uniquely powerful—it's the element of time. Again, pieces of time.

When we made the movie *Hugo* (2011), we went back and tried to recreate that first screening, when people were so startled by the image of an oncoming train that they jumped back. They thought the train was going to hit them.

When we studied the Lumière film, we could see right away that it was very different from the Edison films. The Lumière brothers weren't just setting up the camera to record events or scenes. This film is composed. When you study it, you can see how carefully they placed the camera, the thought that went into what was in the frame and what was left out of the frame, the distance between the camera and the train, the height of the camera, the angle of the camera—what's interesting is that if the camera had been placed even a little bit differently, the audience probably wouldn't have reacted the way it did.

Georges Méliès, whose contribution to early cinema is at the core of *Hugo*, began as a magician and his pictures were made to be a part of his live magic act. He created trick photography and astonishing handmade special effects, and in so doing, he remade reality—the screen in his pictures is like a magic cabinet of curiosities and wonders.

Over the years, the Lumières and Méliès have been consistently portrayed as opposites—the idea is that one filmed reality and the other created special effects. Of course, this kind of distinction is made all the time—it's a way of simplifying history. But in essence they were both heading in the same direction, just taking different roads—they were taking reality and interpreting it, reshaping it, and trying to find meaning in it.

And then, everything was taken further with the cut. Who made the first cut from one image to another—meaning a shift from one vantage point to another with the understanding that we're still within one continuous action? Again, to quote Thomas Mann—"unfathomable." One of the earliest and most famous examples of a cut is in Edwin S. Porter's 1903 milestone film *The Great Train Robbery*. Even though we cut from the interior of the car to the exterior, we know we're in one unbroken action.

A few years later, there was a remarkable film called *The Musketeers of Pig Alley*, one of the dozens of one-reel films that D.W. Griffith made in 1912. It's commonly referred to as the first gangster film, and actually, it's a great Lower East Side New York street film, despite the fact that it was shot in Fort Lee, New Jersey. There's a very famous scene in which the gangsters move along a wall, each one slowly approaching the camera and coming into dramatic close-up before they exit the frame. And in this scene, they're crossing quite a bit of space before they get to Pig Alley, which is in fact a recreation of a famous Jacob Riis photo of Bandit's Roost, but you're not seeing them cross that space on the screen. You're seeing it all in your mind's eye, you're inferring it. And this is the fourth aspect of cinema that's so special. That inference. The image in the mind's eye.

———————————

For me it's where the obsession began. It's what keeps me going, it never fails to excite me. Because you take one shot, you put it together with another shot, and you experience a third image in your mind's eye that doesn't really exist in those two other images. The Soviet filmmaker Sergei Eisenstein wrote about this, and it was at the heart of what he did in his own films. This is what fascinates me—sometimes it's frustrating, but always exciting—if you change the timing of the cut even slightly, by just a few frames, or even one frame, then that third image in your mind's eye changes too. And that has been called, appropriately, I believe, film language.

In 1916, D.W. Griffith made a picture—an epic—called *Intolerance*, in part as an act of atonement for the racism in *The Birth of a Nation*. *Intolerance* ran about three hours and Griffith goes much further with the idea of the cut here: he shifts between four different stories—the massacre of the Huguenots, the passion of Christ, the fall of Babylon, and a modern story set in 1916 about conflicts between rich and poor Americans. At the end of the picture, Griffith cut between the different climaxes of these different stories—he cross-cut through time, something that had never been done before. He tied together images not for narrative purposes but to illustrate a thesis: in this case, the thesis was that intolerance has existed throughout the ages and that it is always destructive. Eisenstein later wrote about this kind of editing and gave it a name—he called it "intellectual montage."

For the writers and commentators who were very suspicious of movies—because after all they did start as a Nickelodeon storefront attraction—this was the element that signified film as an art form. But of course it already was an art form—one that started with the Lumières and Méliès and Porter. This was just another, logical step in

Georges Méliès, circa 1929, with a painting for his 1902 film *A Trip to the Moon* **Image**: Photofest

the development of the language of cinema.

That language has taken us in many directions, from the pure abstraction of the extraordinary avant-garde filmmaker Stan Brakhage to a very well done commercial by the visual artist and filmmaker Mike Mills, made for an audience that's seen thousands of commercials—the images come at you so fast that you have to make the connections after the fact.

Or consider the famous Stargate sequence from Stanley Kubrick's monumental *2001: A Space Odyssey*. Narrative, abstraction, speed, movement, stillness, life, death—they're all up there. Again, we find ourselves back at that mystical urge—to explore, to create movement, to go faster and faster and maybe find some kind of peace at the heart of it, a state of pure being.

But the cinema we're talking about here—Edison, the Lumière brothers, Méliès, Porter, all the way through Griffith and on to Kubrick—that's really almost gone. It's been overwhelmed by moving images coming at us all the time and absolutely everywhere, even faster than the visions coming at the astronaut in the Kubrick picture. And we have no choice but to treat all these moving images coming at us as a language. We need to be able to understand what we're seeing and find the tools to sort it all out.

We certainly agree now that verbal literacy is necessary. But a couple of thousand years ago, Socrates actually disagreed. His argument was almost identical to the arguments of people today who object to the Internet, who think that it's a sorry replacement for real research in a library. In the dialogue with Phaedrus, Socrates worries that writing and reading will actually lead to the student not truly knowing—that once people stop memorising and start writing and reading, they're in danger of cultivating the mere appearance of wisdom rather than the real thing.

Now we take reading and writing for granted but the same kinds of questions are coming up around moving images: Are they harming us? Are they causing us to abandon written language?

We're face to face with images all the time in a way that we never have been before. And that's why I believe we need to stress visual literacy in our schools. Young people need to understand that not all images are there to be consumed like fast food and then forgotten—we need to educate them to understand the difference between moving images that engage their humanity and their intelligence, and moving images that are just selling them something.

As Steve Apkon, the film producer and founder of the Jacob Burns Film Center in Pleasantville, New York, points out in his new book *The Age of the Image*, the distinction between verbal and visual literacy needs to be done away with, along with the tired old arguments about the word and the image and which is more important. They're both important. They're both fundamental. Both take us back to the core of who we are.

When you look at ancient writing, words and images are almost indistinguishable. In fact, words are images, they're symbols. Written Chinese and Japanese still seem like pictographic languages. And at a certain point— exactly when is "unfathomable"— words and images diverged, like two rivers, or two different paths to understanding.

In the end, there really is only literacy.

————————————

The American film critic Manny Farber said that every movie transmits the DNA of its time. One of the really great science fiction films of the golden era of American cinema is Robert Wise's *The Day the Earth Stood Still.* It was made in 1951, in the early years of the cold war, and it has the tension, the paranoia, the fear of nuclear disaster, and the end of life on planet earth, and a million other elements that are more difficult to put into words. These elements have to do with the play of light and shadow, the emotional and psychological interplay between the characters, the atmosphere of the time woven into the action, all the choices that were made behind the camera that resulted in the immediate film experience for viewers like myself and my parents. These are the aspects of a film that reveal themselves in passing, the things that bring the movie to life for the viewer. And the experience becomes even richer when you explore these elements more closely.

Someone born today will see the picture with completely different eyes and a whole other frame of reference, different values, uninhibited by the biases of the time when it was made. You see the world through your own time— which means that some values disappear, and some values come into closer focus. Same film, same images, but in the case of a great film the power—a timeless power that really can't be articulated—is there even when the context has completely changed.

But in order to experience something and find new values in it, the work has to be there in the first place—you have to preserve it. All of it. Archaeologists have made many discoveries by studying what we throw away, the refuse of earlier civilisations, the things that people considered expendable and that accidentally survived.

For example, there's a Sumerian tablet that is not a poem, not a legend, but actually a record of livestock—a balance sheet of business transactions. Miraculously, it's been preserved for centuries, first under layers of earth and now in a climate-controlled environment. When we find objects like this, we immediately take great care with them.

We have to do the same thing with film. But film isn't made of stone. Until recently, it was all made of celluloid—thin strips of nitrocellulose, the first plastic compound. For the first few decades of cinema, preservation wasn't even discussed—it was something that happened by accident. Some of the most celebrated movies were the victims of their own popularity. In certain cases, every time they were rereleased, the prints were made from their original negatives, and in the process, those negatives became degraded, hardly usable.

It wasn't so long ago that nitrate films were melted down just for the silver content. Prints of films made in the 1970s and 1980s were recycled to make guitar picks and plastic heels for shoes. That's a disturbing thought—just as disturbing as knowing that many of those extraordinary glass photographic plates taken of the Civil War not long after the birth of photography were later sold to gardeners for building greenhouses. Whatever plates survived are now in the Library of Congress.

We have to look beyond the officially honoured, recognised, and enshrined, and preserve everything systematically. At this point in film history, many people have seen a 1958 picture directed by Alfred Hitchcock called *Vertigo.* When the film came out some people liked it, some didn't, and then it just went away. Even before it came out, it was classified as another picture from the Master of Suspense, and that was it, end of story. Almost every year at that time, there was a new Hitchcock picture—it was almost like a franchise.

At a certain point, there was a re-evaluation of Hitchcock, thanks to the critics in France who later became the directors of the French New Wave, and to the American critic Andrew Sarris. They all enhanced our vision of cinema and helped us to understand the idea of authorship *behind* the camera. When the idea of film language started to be taken seriously, so did Hitchcock, who seemed to have an innate sense of visual storytelling. And the more closely you looked at his pictures, the richer and more emotionally complex they became.

For many years, it was extremely difficult to see *Vertigo.* When it came back into circulation, in 1983, along with four other Hitchcock films that had been held back, the colour was completely wrong. The colour scheme of *Vertigo* is extremely unusual, and this was a major disappointment. In the meantime, the elements—the original picture and sound negatives—needed serious attention.

Ten years later, Bob Harris and Jim Katz did a full-scale restoration for Universal. By that time, the elements were decaying and severely damaged. But at least a major restoration was done. As the years went by, more and more people saw *Vertigo* and came to appreciate its hypnotic beauty and very strange, obsessive focus.

———————————

As in the case of many great films, maybe all of them, we don't keep going back for the plot. *Vertigo* is a matter of mood as much as it's a matter of storytelling—the special mood of San Francisco where the past is eerily alive and around you at all times, the mist in the air from the Pacific that refracts the light, the unease of the hero played by James Stewart, Bernard Herrmann's haunting score. As the film critic B. Kite wrote, you haven't really seen *Vertigo* until you've seen it *again*. For those of you who haven't seen it even once, when you do, you'll know what I mean.

Every decade, the British film magazine *Sight and Sound* conducts a poll of critics and filmmakers from around the world and asks them to list what they think are the ten greatest films of all time. Then they tally the results and publish them. In 1952, number one was Vittorio de Sica's great Italian Neorealist picture *Bicycle Thieves*. Ten years later, Orson Welles's *Citizen Kane* was at the top of the list. It stayed there for the next forty years. Last year, it was displaced by a movie that came and went in 1958, and that came very, very close to being lost to us forever: *Vertigo*. And by the way, so did *Citizen Kane*—the original negative was burned in a fire in the mid-1970s in Los Angeles.

So not only do we have to preserve everything, but most importantly, we can't afford to let ourselves be guided by contemporary cultural standards—particularly now. There was a time when the average person wasn't even aware of box-office grosses. But since the 1980s, it's become a kind of sport—and really, a form of judgment. It culturally trivialises film.

And for young people today, that's what they know. Who made the most money? Who was the most popular? Who is the most popular now, as opposed to last year, or last month, or last week? Now, the cycles of popularity are down to a matter of hours, minutes, seconds, and the work that's been created out of seriousness and real passion is lumped together with the work that hasn't.

We have to remember: we may think we know what's going to last and what isn't. We may feel absolutely sure of ourselves, but we really don't know, we *can't* know. We have to remember *Vertigo*, and the Civil War plates, and that Sumerian tablet. And we also have to remember that *Moby Dick* sold very few copies when it was printed in 1851, that many of the copies that weren't sold were destroyed in a warehouse fire, that it was dismissed by many, and that Herman Melville's greatest novel, one of the greatest works in literature, was only reclaimed in the 1920s.

Just as we've learned to take pride in our poets and writers, in jazz and the blues, we need to take pride in our cinema, our great American art form. Granted, we weren't the only ones who invented the movies. We certainly weren't the only ones who made great films in the twentieth century, but to a large extent, the art of cinema and its development have been linked to us, to our country. That's a big responsibility. And we need to say to ourselves that the moment has come when we have to treat every last moving image as reverently and respectfully as the oldest book in the Library of Congress.

Martin Scorsese is an American filmmaker, producer and film preservationist. He is the founder of The Film Foundation, a nonprofit organisation dedicated to film preservation.

© Martin Scorsese. Reprinted courtesy The New York Review of Books and the National Endowment for the Humanities 42nd Jefferson Lecture.

THE CONSERVATION
OF MOVING IMAGES

PAOLO CHERCHI USAI

An unidentified reel of 35 mm film in a terminal stage of decomposition **Courtesy**: George Eastman House

In the late 1920s, a major European manufacturer of motion picture film stock, Agfa (Aktiengesellschaft für Anilinfabrikation), published a multi-volume promotional book showcasing actual samples of 35 mm negative and positive frames on a nitrate cellulose base. The condition of the extant copies is often astonishing. The sharpness, translucency and vibrancy of the images is matched by the pristine condition of their 'photochemical' carriers.

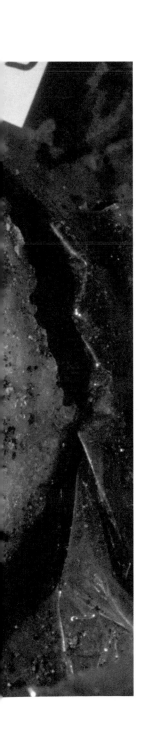

Other companies in Europe and the United States—notably Pathé and Eastman Kodak—produced similar booklets exhibiting their products. Many of them are still excellently preserved, although their quality can hardly be compared with that of their German competitor. Several prints and negatives of films produced between 1896 and 1908 by the French firms Lumière and Pathé, by the British company Mitchell & Kenyon, and by the Biograph Company of New York are in such good shape that they could be safely handled with the appropriate equipment.

What is so special about the Agfa frames, however, is that they make us acutely aware of a lost opportunity; had they been stored in ideal conditions of temperature and humidity from the moment of their creation, the films they document could probably have been projected today. Their progressive obliteration in the ensuing decades was a likely, but not inevitable, event. According to informal estimates established by the members of the International Federation of Film Archives (FIAF), approximately 80% of the films produced during the so-called 'silent era' (1894–1930) are now considered to be lost.

There are, of course, compelling reasons why the destruction occurred. Cellulose nitrate film was the main carrier of 'photochemical' moving images until it was commercially replaced by cellulose triacetate film—a carrier also prone to a form of chemical decomposition known as 'vinegar syndrome'. Acetate-based film had been used at least since 1912 for Chronochrome, a colour system on 35 mm film commissioned to the Eastman Kodak company by the French producer Léon Gaumont; diacetate and triacetate film were used on a larger scale after 1920 for non-theatrical formats such as 16 mm films. Acetate-based film was, in turn, replaced by polyester film in the early 1990s for release prints. It is worth noting that acetate-based film is still in use for original camera negatives; this is due to the fact that the much higher tensile strength of polyester film may cause damage to the camera equipment if it is incorrectly threaded within the machine. Cellulose nitrate film stock is chemically unstable, but so are many other artefacts of cultural value.

Motion picture film was—and still is, even in its current incarnation on a polyester base—meant to be discarded after use, but this also applies to other and much older works exhibited in museums. A short film by Paolo Lipari, *Due dollari al chilo* (2000), shows a machine for shredding 35 mm feature films after their commercial distribution. The equipment, known as 'the guillotine'

A machine for shredding 35 mm feature films after their commercial distribution. Frame enlargement from a 35 mm polyester print of *Due dollari al chilo* (Paolo Lipari, 2000). Author's collection.

and located in Cinisello Balsamo near Milan, Italy, was known to shred over 150000 prints of polyester film per year in 1999, sent from all parts of Europe. The stock is converted into low-cost fuel for electricity generation, and raw materials for benches, combs, spectacle frames and clothing. A similar plant in Millesimo, also in Italy, was dedicated to the recycling of triacetate cellulose film.

THE FIELD OF MOVING IMAGE CONSERVATION

For a long time, the moving image was not regarded as an art form, but the same can be said of countless items now displayed in public and private collections all over the world. The presumed difference between cinema and other types of aesthetic expression relied upon two basic assumptions: first, that film is progressively altered by the very act of its presentation by means of a machine; second, that the creative works it embodies are subject to reproduction from a master copy, and that new copies can be made at will, thus making the conservation of the individual print unnecessary. The intrinsic flaw in these seemingly uncontroversial statements lies not in the arguments themselves, but in their unquestioning reliance on quantitative variables. All human-made objects deteriorate in time, whether by usage—a pot, a piece of jewellery—or through exposure to their normal environment. The distinction lies in the rate of decay: millennia for ceramics (if they are not broken), centuries for paintings and frescoes, decades for an unprotected daguerreotype. Etchings, albumen photographic prints and Babylonian seals were also made from matrices; the survival or disappearance of the latter does not affect the value attributed to copies made from them before their acquisition by a collecting institution.

The closest equivalents to motion picture film in this respect are magic lantern slides and phonograph discs. Like film, they were produced in multiple copies; like film, every viewing or listening event involved some wear and tear of the carrier; like film, they cannot be experienced without an apparatus—which is where any useful comparison between moving images and most of the other arts seems to fall apart. Magic lantern specialists have begun to discuss informally whether or not it is preferable, or even advisable, to show original glass slides as opposed to analog or digital reproductions. The option of playing (on special occasions) original phonograph discs instead of reproductions of their sound recordings is occasionally discussed in recorded sound archives, but no technology for analog preservation on a mass scale is currently available to them. The field of moving image conservation is taking yet another approach, influenced by at least two popular lines of thought. The first view—by far, the most common—is that cinema is regarded primarily as entertainment, the product of an industry providing audiovisual 'content' to consumers worldwide. This leads to the opinion that those who view moving images are indifferent to—or unaware of—the technology adopted for this purpose, thus providing a rationale for preserving films on whatever media are available at the lowest cost.

The second presumption—encouraged in the academic world by a superficial reading of Walter Benjamin's canonical essay *Das Kunstwerk im Zeitalter seiner technischen Reproduzierbarkeit* (1936)—is that the lack of an 'aura' of uniqueness in the traditional photographic film gives no incentive to treat the copy in question as an artefact, thereby endorsing the view that a damaged item can always be replaced with an identical copy. The consequences of this approach to the conservation of moving images as part of the cultural heritage have been profound. The physical deterioration of film has been taken for granted not only in the commercial circuit but also in archives and museums, to the point that the creation of a so-called preservation element—for instance, an intermediate negative—has been implicitly regarded as a suitable response to the 'inevitable' mistreatment of the projection copy: when a film becomes unusable, all that is needed is to copy another one from the master. Much of the damage to copies occurs during projection and shipping, but because they are deemed to be ephemeral by default, there is little or no real commitment to establishing stricter rules for their correct curatorial treatment. Recent attempts to implement procedures and protocols derived from standard museum practice in other areas have generally been unsuccessful. An exception is George Eastman House, which has adopted an open- source 'facility condition report' to be submitted by borrowing institutions before the loan of an archival print.

THE IMPACT OF DIGITAL TECHNOLOGY

The advent of digital technology has brought a further twist to this issue by giving film museums and archives the illusion that the problem is over, in the sense that the conversion of the analog photographic image into a digital file would bypass the 'integrity' dilemma altogether: no more wear and tear on the print, and no more necessity to worry about its material condition. This too is an illusion, as digital files can easily be corrupted. What changes is only the 'object' of decay—digital data instead of a semi-transparent base or a gelatin emulsion. Given that, allegedly, film is an art of reproduction, the audience does not care how it is exhibited as long as it 'looks good' on the screen, and as a digital carrier is reportedly easier to keep intact, why bother insisting on its permanent availability on its original medium? This attitude towards the conservation of the moving image has engendered a great deal of confusion over what digital techniques can and cannot achieve. 'Digitisation' has become a catchword encompassing three very different processes, goals and objectives. Not all of them can be achieved through the same means. It is worth describing what they are.

Digital restoration is the overall set of technical and curatorial procedures aimed at making the moving image appear (by means of digital image manipulation or processing) as close as possible to what it presumably was at the time of its original release, or according to the intentions of its maker. The tools available to film preservation professionals in the digital domain have enabled them to achieve what would have seemed impossible with traditional photographic chemical methods: colour, contrast and image stability can be greatly improved (more faith-

fully to the original or, problematically, even beyond) with techniques previously unimaginable in the 'analog' laboratory. This is one of the great advantages of digital techniques; a responsible use of this resource can successfully complement the 'analog' restoration process, whose prerogatives are also unique and distinct from their digital counterparts.

Digitisation is the process of converting analog photographic material into digital files for the purposes of public access. This is the great promise of digital technology: in theory, hundreds of thousands of films produced by traditional photographic means can be made accessible to a much wider audience in a variety of formats. Digitisation does not equal digital restoration, in the sense that 'analog' moving images are turned into digital files, regardless of their original condition. A 'digitised' moving image is not necessarily 'restored'.

Digital preservation entails a technological infrastructure capable of making the 'digitised' and 'digitally restored' moving image permanently available for viewing. According to many specialists in the industry and in collecting institutions, there is no such infrastructure at the present time, in the sense that there is no known technique for ensuring that the restored or digitised moving images will remain intact for an indefinite future. The two main obstacles facing moving image archivists and curators are the need to periodically migrate the digital files, and the rapid obsolescence of the equipment used for storing them. A groundbreaking report titled *The Digital Dilemma* declares that

> In the motion picture industry, there is a major difference between an archive and a library. The archive holds master-level content in preservation conditions with long-term access capability. A library is a temporary storage site, circulating its duplicated holdings on demand. An archive that stores digital materials has long-term objectives. By current practice and definition, digital storage is short-term... more than 100 years after its introduction, 35 mm film is the shining example of a standardised and sustainable format that is widely adopted, globally inter-operable, stable, and well understood ... if we allow the historical phenomenon of technological obsolescence to repeat itself, we are tied either to continuously increasing costs—or worse—the failure to save important assets. [Science and Technology Council of the Academy of Motion Picture Arts and Sciences, *The Digital Dilemma*, 2007]

An employee of the Douglas Fairbanks Studio chopping up 'useless' film (1922). **Courtesy:** National Center for Film and Video Preservation.

The problem with this terminology is that the distinction it suggests is too subtle to be understood or appreciated by a non-specialised audience and by the funding bodies of collecting institutions. For both constituencies, 'digitisation' means everything: conservation (safeguarding forever), restoration (making vintage films look new), immediate and unlimited access (here, now, at any time). The confusion is compounded by the fact that there is no consensus on the very definition of preservation, restoration and conservation among moving image specialists. At a purely theoretical level, the act of digital migration fulfils at the same time the goal of protecting 'content' *and* enabling its widest dissemination in a form as pristine as it was originally made. However, this reductionist approach fails to account for the inherently ephemeral nature of the digital formats, their vulnerability to data corruption, and the impossibility of exercising full intellectual control over an almost infinite body of works in constant, exponential growth.

The terminology suggested above also assumes that 'digital' is the only way in which the cinematic heritage will be preserved in the immediate future. There are plenty of indicators supporting this view, beginning with the fact that cinema itself is taking the digital route. in May 2010, the Norsk Filminstitutt (Norwegian Film Institute) announced that Norway's cinema network (85 theatres) would switch in its entirety to digital projection, stating that Norway is the first country in the world to take this measure; 35 mm projection equipment is to be maintained in selected venues and in cinemas where there is also enough room for analog machines in the projection booth. On the other hand, the imminent demise of analog film projection on a global scale has been predicted for more than a decade, but it has not yet fully happened. It will eventually, although there are convincing signs pointing in directions other than 'digital'. The film industry has recognised that conservation on analog, silver halide-based photographic materials is still the most reliable way of making sure that moving images produced today will still be available in the foreseeable future, and it is common practice among mainstream production and distribution companies to keep analog masters of films originally produced or released in digital form. Their prudence in managing the digital revolution they have themselves promoted should be treated as a cautionary tale for collecting institutions.

There will soon be a time when all moving images will be born digital, and their long-term conservation will be the object of yet another challenge for preservation professionals. Meanwhile, film museums and archives will be facing two major questions. Will there be a role for them as caretakers of the world's (digital) audiovisual heritage? And, what will they do with the finite but huge corpus of moving images produced in analog form? The two agendas are different, but complementary in their essence. It is generally accepted, albeit reluctantly—even within the film industry community—that the best way to protect the integrity of a 35 mm film is to duplicate it onto another 35 mm carrier or group of carriers, and to keep the masters under strictly monitored environmental conditions, involving cold storage and controlled humidity. It has been stated that

> Preservation planning should now emphasise a balanced approach which combines duplication and improved storage. In the long term, improved storage is by far the most cost-effective and satisfactory solution... the most important new element in preservation planning is the realisation that safety films are more sensitive to poor storage than previously thought, requiring better conditions, careful monitoring and active collection management. [Reilly, J.M., Adelstein, P.Z., and Nishimura, D.W., *Preservation of Safety Film*, 1991].

Although the Hollywood majors are doing it, even with digital-born films, non-profit collecting institutions cannot necessarily afford such a luxury and in most cases have given up all hope of preserving systematically their entire cinematic legacy in analog form. The most they can do is keep the films intact as much as they can, follow best practice for a limited number of key items and 'digitise' (in the broadest sense of the term) all the rest. In doing so, they have to cope with an endemic lack of funding and with the political pressure to embrace the digital route: from the point of view of a government, 'digital' equals public consensus, and therefore improved chances of re-election of the ruling party or coalition. 'Digitising' everything, properly preserving the masterworks and keeping the analog films in warehouses at temperatures below freezing point is the threefold strategy that has emerged in moving image archives and museums at the dawn of this century.

It is a flawed, contradictory and dangerous route, but it is better than having no strategy at all. However, when it comes to digital-born moving images, another dilemma emerges. Safeguarding everything? How? And if 'everything' (whatever that means in the digital domain) can actually be protected, what kind of intellectual framework will enable archives and museums to distinguish themselves from the many other 'content providers' proliferating on the Internet? It may well be that the solution adopted by *force majeure* for the traditional analog collections (that is, selecting the most representative or outstanding works on the basis of curatorial judgment) will need to be applied—with the required amendments—to the digital collections as well.

THE WAY FORWARD

No matter what, the time of reckoning has come for what used to be called 'film archives' and 'museums'. Under the present circumstances, there is no guarantee that these institutions will be allowed to continue their mission within the remit they created for themselves in the twentieth century. If they wish to have a future, they will need to provide clear answers to a number of key questions which they have evaded so far, either because of an inevitable fear of the unknown, or because of a perceived risk of alienating their internal and external stakeholders. For the sake of further discussion, it is worth trying to formulate these points as clearly as possible.

First, governments and funding agencies should be made aware that the systematic and comprehensive digital restoration of all analog moving images in a major collecting institution is simply not possible in practical terms. The amount of money and personnel required for such a daunting task goes way beyond the most optimistic forecast of the financial resources available to the cultural sector. While there is a remote possibility that this could successfully happen with digital-born images, the costs of creating (and maintaining) a dedicated infrastructure for the purpose are not proportionate to the likely outcome, and it is a mistake to pretend otherwise. The public will not have unlimited access to a national audiovisual collection in the same way it does to a national library. Any financial effort aimed at conveying this feeling of omnipotence is a waste of public support which would be better channelled toward a responsible and selective curatorial management of the collections. As far as the analog motion picture heritage is concerned, a national film archive will never be able to compete with the private sector on a quantitative basis.

It is in qualitative terms that a difference can be made, both by providing a more thorough understanding of the collections and by promoting the collecting institution as a cultural authority. If it makes sense for a collecting institution to be the last place on earth where moving images are kept and shown in the way they used to be, a state-of-the-art film preservation laboratory (analog and digital) and a regular exhibition programme of superior quality for cinema (analog and digital) will be as important as a well-considered and responsibly maintained digital network.

Second, it is imperative for everyone—audiences, curators, funding agencies—to be aware of the archive's philosophical position on the material status of the pre-digital portion of the collection. Why are we preserving it at all?

There are legitimate arguments for protecting it just because an 'analog' print is the most reliable physical evidence of a film, or because its survival represents the historical pathway of a past technology to be studied by future generations. A print in 35 mm format may just be a convenient source for duplication onto other media, but it could also be the carrier of a distinctive visual phenomenon, different (not better or worse—just different) from the experience conveyed through the electronic image. Are we committed to protect this uniqueness as an aesthetic principle, or as part of a business plan, or merely as a matter of nostalgia? Do we want people to care about the revival of a 35 mm projection as a curatorial performance, as an archaeological trace, or as an object of curiosity similar, say, to the prototype of a steam engine or to the tools used for a fourteenth-century woodcut? Any of these ways are fine, as long as we say so clearly, unequivocally and with a solid, persuasive rationale.

Third, it makes sense to say, publicly and unambiguously, whether moving images are being preserved for their 'content', or for the overall cultural context they represent. In the former case, the way in which these images are preserved and made accessible is irrelevant, and there is no need to keep a print on photographic motion picture film stock for reasons other than its proven longevity under adequate storage conditions. In the latter case, curators must accept the responsibility to ensure that the audience in the late twenty-first century will be able to view moving images in the same way as they were seen at the time of their creation. It is important to note that this concern is pertinent well beyond the cinema, video and television programmes made in the pre-digital era. A collecting institution specialising in moving images should be as committed to the presentation of a 35 mm print on a Kinetoscope made in 1894 as to showing how moving image files were seen on an iPod manufactured in 2001. Neither apparatus will be commercially available in 3010, but this is not a good enough reason to discount the significance of being able to exhibit them long after the technologies they represent are defunct.

Film preservation professionals have argued for the distinctive nature of the moving image as opposed to other forms of aesthetic and cultural expression, and tried at the same time to assert their legitimacy by presenting themselves as worthy of acceptance in the art conservation world, without being able or willing to take the full consequences of their ambition. Not surprisingly, neither the 'fine arts' community nor the 'arts and crafts' world have really treated the cinema or electronic image constituencies as their peers, except occasionally for the sheer convenience of hosting audiovisual works in gallery installations. One of the great conundrums in the moving image curatorial field is that in order to be admitted to a museum gallery, cinema was forced—to put it mildly— to reinvent itself in electronic or digital form in order to be taken seriously; in other words, a mode of expression had to adapt itself to the exhibition space rather than vice versa.

The effects of this mutual uneasiness in the field of conservation are paradoxical, to say the least. Curators of the fine arts exhibit videos reproducing films of the early twentieth century as ancillary evidence of a painting style, but they also acquire (often for large sums of money) digital works which they regard as unique, even though their permanence will be dependent upon the ongoing migration of the data on other carriers; a duty they delegate happily to their information technology departments. Conversely, moving image archivists and curators are keen to flirt with museum practice without truly engaging with it beyond some perfunctory statements of intent. As the unspoken mantra goes: it is a good idea to treat 35 mm film prints very carefully, but never mind if they are shipped in cardboard containers; ensure that the best image quality is achieved during the conservation process, but don't worry if the print gets scratched or otherwise damaged by an untrained projectionist.

As this self-defeating attitude is so engrained in curators' minds, the advent of digital technology gives them the perfect excuse to bypass the issue of conservation and museum practice altogether, without having engaged with it at all: a digital file doesn't get scratched, therefore there is no longer any need to worry about it as an object, which amounts to a *de facto* abdication of responsibility. There is something ironic in this unconscious and yet pervasive attitude toward the moving image artefact: the more it loses its status of 'material' (or, worse, it is treated as a costly liability because of the effort needed to keep it in a refrigerated vault), the more enthusiastically it is legitimised as a cultural phenomenon. On the one hand, recent literature in film preservation prides itself on repeatedly using the term 'ethics', and has grown accustomed to quoting the works of Cesare Brandi as a source of inspiration; on the other hand, not only is film virtually absent from specialist publications on the conservation of the cultural heritage, but film preservation professionals have yet to demonstrate much interest in hosting specialised research from experts in other domains within their conferences and periodicals.

This mutual indifference was never justifiable on the grounds of academic integrity—even at a time when cinema was a second-class citizen as far as academic curricula were concerned—and it is indefensible on pragmatic grounds, given the currently increasing cross-pollination between the arts. Moving-image curators and conservation professionals have no good reason for discounting what is happening in the other curatorial areas, and no longer deserve to be ignored by them. Both have failed to explain to each other—let alone to non-specialists—why they share the same concerns. It is time to reverse the trend and open the doors to a rigorous, constructive and non-antagonistic dialogue between the parties. Whether the parties are willing and able to do so is, of course, another matter.

This is an abridged and revised version of an essay originally published as 'The Conservation of Moving Images', in Studies in Conservation, *vol. 55, no. 4, 2010, pp. 250-257. It is reproduced here by kind permission of the author and the publisher.*

Paolo Cherchi Usai is the Senior Curator of the Motion Picture Department at George Eastman House in Rochester, NY. He teaches film preservation and has written several books on cinema.

FILM FOREVER?

DAVID WALSH

Nitrate film storage, built at a time when safety was considered more important than low temperature. **Image:** IWM

The Iron Pillar of Delhi is well over a thousand years old, and yet remains uncorroded due to the unusual constitution of the iron from which it was forged. We do not expect film to have this kind of resilience. Even relatively stable silver images on polyester film are unlikely to survive without considerable protection from the elements. And there is a second essential for survival over the very long term: chance.

For all its resistance to rust, the iron pillar could easily have been lost, buried or broken up, as indeed have whole cities in this time. The pillar is there for all to see through a happy combination of good fortune and a freak of metallurgy. So although film manufacturers may claim a thousand-year lifetime for a film archive's precious assets if they are stored in the right conditions, the element of luck will still play a major part in whether there will be anything viable to dig out of the rubble of our civilisation once the barbarian hordes have swept through. Film is certainly not forever.

What then is the life expectancy of a film? Are we hoping for archaeological timescales? If so, then our best bet is to fill cool and dry caves with black-and-white polyester films (in an initiative similar to the Global Seed Vault in Svalbard in the Arctic), so that some of them will survive to be chanced upon by future civilisations. The good thing about planning on this timescale is that we will never know whether it has been successful or not.

In truth, though, archaeological preservation is just too difficult, costly and chancy, and we have to accept that most of the film in the world's archives will simply rot away once there is no longer any caretaker to keep the flame alive. In the very real world that film archives operate in, the best that most archivists can hope for is that we don't make too much of a mess of things for the next couple of generations. This is not so much a dereliction of duty as an acknowledgement that we really have no idea what the distant future holds. But in order to avoid messing things up for our successors, we have to take action now. The problem is determining what that action should be.

A good starting point is that we should not do anything irreversible if it can be avoided, and among other things this means that the originals should not be destroyed, this being the most irreversible process of them all. This leads to the simplest and purest approach to film preservation, which is to keep the original films in ideal storage and do nothing else. This approach is not as straightforward as it may seem. Black-and-white polyester film may survive happily enough in moderate conditions, provided the atmosphere is relatively dry, but most film originals are less resilient, being either colour, or supported on altogether less robust types of plastic. Such films, especially if they are already old and declining, are unlikely to survive for long if left in inadequate storage, and even if some do, they will require careful restoration and recovery work in order to make the sound and images once again fit for an audience. The flip side to this gloomy prospect is that proper archival cold storage (generally below zero Celsius) will reliably safeguard these films for future generations—provided they have not already degraded too far.

Why then is this policy of proper storage not universally adopted by film archives around the world? The most obvious reason is money: even the most compelling argument (that we will lose all our films) counts for little or nothing in the reality of short-term public sector or commercial spending. Pointing out that it will be ten times as expensive to restore all the films which have faded away than it would be to store them properly so that they don't, is likely to elicit the response that, well, there will never be any money for restoration either.

A quick survey of those archives which do achieve the recommended storage conditions shows that most of them are from rich countries in temperate regions. It is not hard to see why: a preservation policy has to be affordable and effective. In temperate regions, most of the collection, even after years of neglect and inadequate storage, is likely to be still viable. At the same time, expertise in designing efficient and reliable cold and dry storage has advanced greatly recently, so that, if the outside conditions are not so extreme, such stores have become reasonably affordable and sustainable. Nevertheless, it is a big commitment, even where the money exists for cultural spending on this scale.

Move to a country such as India, with an often hot and damp climate, where there are so many more urgencies demanding public money, and where large parts of film collections have already degraded to a point where the original is beyond hope, and the situation is less rosy. What is the answer here? Build a climate-controlled, sub-zero store powered somehow by a local renewable source? This may be perfectly possible, even where the outside temperature soars and the humidity is way above the point that fungus will delight in devouring the gelatine in the emulsion. But it is not cheap, and there is compelling anecdotal evidence that film which has already degraded beyond a critical point will continue to decompose appreciably even at sub-zero temperatures; good storage is simply too late for these films. The archivist unlucky enough to be working in such an archive is inevitably caught by both issues: it's too expensive to run suitably climate-controlled vaults and there is a legacy of deteriorated films way beyond any help from any kind of storage.

Nonetheless, many archivists take the uncompromising stance that the original films cannot be destroyed; they must be stored for as long as possible. In principle, they are absolutely correct. However, it must be understood that there cannot be any compromise on the conditions. They must be fully up to the recommended standards for the type and condition of the films, otherwise the archive is merely condemning the films to eventual destruction under the pretence of preserving them.

And if we can't properly preserve the original film in our vaults, what is the solution? Anyone familiar with traditional film preservation, where the terms 'preservation' and 'copying' were often synonymous, will know the answer to this, which is to make a stable copy of the original which can be preserved in place of the original. It is important to understand that the moment the archive starts making preservation copies, it is setting out on a path away from authenticity, since only the original films can be truly authentic. Any copying process is imperfect, whether it is photochemical or digital; both are subject to limitations in the technology and the skill of the operators, and the result may end up some distance from the original in terms of faithfulness.

Assuming there is a necessity to make a preservation copy, the next question is how? The answer is tangled: in terms of resolution, a high-quality digital scan is broadly as good as a photochemical copy made on a traditional film printer, but faithful copying of an analog medium such as film is subject to all kinds of other factors beyond mere resolution. Both photochemical and digital copying rely on complex processes whose outcomes may be difficult to predict, and the end result is highly dependent on the equipment used, the skill of the operators and the degree of care taken. A specialist film laboratory with expert technicians and with enough time and money can, using photochemical means, produce really good copies from less-than-perfect originals. However, this tends to be the preserve of a few very well-resourced archives, and such traditional expertise is now becoming a thing of the past. Archivists are discovering that it is much easier (and cheaper) to get a satisfactory result when copying digitally than by making a photochemical copy (both for the picture and the sound). On balance, digital copying, despite its flaws and provided it is done competently and at a suitable resolution, is the better way of making a preservation master in the majority of cases—as long as it is remembered that this is still a poor substitute for preserving the original.

Of course, there is far more to preservation than the quality of the preservation master. A superior digital copy is of no use if our successors can't retrieve and open it, and it is in terms of life expectancy that film's apparent supremacy is most often championed. The lifetime of modern black-and-white film in appropriate storage is predicted to be many hundreds of years, but as with everything connected with film preservation, things aren't quite as simple as they might at first seem. What if the original film is in colour? Although it is a well-established process to capture each of the three primary colours on separate black-and-white films which can then be preserved in relatively mild storage conditions, it is very expensive to do this, and requires three times as much storage space. If instead the archive decides to make a single preservation copy on colour stock, they are back at square one—they need below-zero storage to preserve it, otherwise the lifetime of the colour dyes will be seriously compromised.

How do the prospects for film compare with the life expectancy of digital data? Framed in this way, the question is unanswerable, since unlike analog film, digital data does not follow a predictable pattern of degradation. Digital data can in theory be kept forever with absolutely no loss of information, but the real issue is how much risk there is of significant loss at any point in the future, and the risk is as high the moment the data is created as it is in years to come. Slightly more predictable is the rate of obsolescence of formats and systems: there have been many scare stories of data lost or rescued just in time as the means to read it becomes outdated and the equipment falls into disuse. But just as it is important to monitor the degradation of vulnerable films, digital preservation can

only work if the technology is constantly under review, and action taken before it is too late. It is this unceasing need to keep the plates spinning which causes the most discomfort for film archivists, accustomed as they are to easily readable artefacts sitting safely on shelves, and this is why recording the digital version back onto film seems so comforting, even though the process inevitably results in a loss of resolution. Some are happy to take this notion a step further and use film as a medium to store the information in the form of digital data rather than an analog image—there have been a number of systems of this sort put forward over the years, and one at least is now a commercial product, though exactly where this approach sits between the best and the worst of both worlds is hard to determine.

At the moment, putting films in cold stores may still be cheaper than secure digital storage, because reducing the risk of total digital loss to an acceptable level (whatever that might be) requires multiple copies in different formats and on different storage media, coupled with carefully worked-out plans (and guaranteed funds) for future migrations to new formats, all of which is beyond the realm of the archivist's traditional area of expertise. But as years go by, low-temperature film storage will continue to cost much the same, depending as it does largely on energy and land prices, while most experts believe that the cost of digital storage will continue to drop steadily, so that in a relatively short time, many believe that it will become cheaper than physical storage. But we are still some way from a position where storing unique-master films digitally will be reliable enough for archives to adopt with real confidence: there is simply too much that can go wrong, and although researchers are working on technologies for passive digital storage which might ultimately lead to a medium that can cheerfully be abandoned in a storeroom for centuries, this is still some way off.

Those of a gloomy disposition might summarise this discussion as follows: if we do everything we can to preserve the original film material, we might end up exhausting all our funds on storage which still fails to secure our films' long-term future; however, if we make a preservation copy, it's not clear whether this should be a photochemical or digital copy, and either way, it will be inferior to the original in quality... and we can't guarantee its future survival anyway. Perhaps, like the films of the silent era, we should resign ourselves to losing an 80-percent chunk of our heritage.

Well, no. Film archiving may not be easy, but it's not

impossible, and it may be digital technology that comes to the rescue, though most likely as an adjunct to film rather than a replacement. We are just arriving at a time where routine digital film copying is becoming a practical reality for archives, whereas hitherto it has been the preserve of high-end restoration projects. The film scanners coming on to the market now are fast, tailored to deal with all varieties of film, and while not exactly cheap, are falling in price. As imaging technology develops, it will literally be possible to scan a film with a mobile phone (although this may not be an ideal practical approach), so doom-laden talk about scanners no longer being available once there is no need for them in film production is misplaced. At the same time, the management of the large files emanating from film scans, where an hour's high-resolution film produces a bloated 4 Terabytes of data, is just beginning to seem less daunting as processor speeds, storage and bandwidths rapidly rise.

Wealthy archives may indeed choose to make black-and-white preservation copies on polyester film, on the grounds that this is the one form that can survive future neglect. But for most of us this is not an option, no matter how much we might wish it otherwise, and as laboratory after laboratory goes out of business, making preservation copies on film will become more and more the exception. There is no doubt that in the past this approach served archives well enough when dealing with nitrate, but even the most dedicated film enthusiast recognises that very many of the preservation masters made were really not very good, even if they have (thank heavens) succeeded in keeping the films alive. And if we are really forced to live without film stock and film laboratories in the future, even the rich archives will no longer have the option of making reasonably robust, if slightly imperfect, film copies capable of being safely abandoned somewhere in a forgotten store.

So what are the preservation options for the film archive of today? The conflict between the affordable and the ideal is always present, made worse by the fact that film archivists often can't agree about what is ideal. Any policy decision we make now imposes obligations on our successors: they will have to keep the cold store, the digital storage, the migration plan all running, and will not thank us if our idea of perfect preservation imposes obligations on them that they cannot meet. We must be guided by how likely it is that the curses of future archivists will be ringing in our long-dead ears.

The table below sets out the most obvious possible policies, bearing in mind that different parts of the collection may need different approaches.

POLICY	ADVANTAGES	DISADVANTAGES
Preserve the originals in appropriate storage	Original quality and authenticity retained	Requires costly stores to be kept running indefinitely
Make film preservation copies and allow the originals to degrade	Relatively mild storage conditions required if B&W copies are made	Expensive to make copies/Quality can be compromised/Requires costly stores if colour copies are made
Preserve the originals in appropriate storage and make digital preservation copies	Originals retained and quality of preservation copies is good	Requires costly storage/Reliability of digital preservation is unknown
Make digital preservation copies and allow originals to degrade	Quality of preservation copies is good/Relatively cheap in the longer term	Risk of complete loss if digital preservation fails

Keeping in mind our objective of not leaving a disastrous legacy for our successors, let us look at these options. The first assumes that the archive already has copies other than the masters which can be used for access, or is prepared to take the masters out of store in order to make on-request access copies (for what is the point of an archive completely closed to access?). There is certainly a lot to be said for this option: the originals are preserved just as they are, and there is no rushing to making digital masters before the technology has really matured. There is of course a considerable risk that some of the films will actually degrade over the coming years, so careful monitoring of vulnerable films is essential. No film will last forever, and sooner or later our successors will have to face the prospect of duplicating the material for preservation, but perhaps by then there will be a reliable automated way of doing this. However, this option is only really viable if most of the film is still in reasonable condition, and if building and running the right kind of stores is feasible.

The second option of making preservation copies on film has a number of disadvantages: whether this is done by photochemical duplication or by recording digital scans back onto film (itself a lossy process), the quality may be compromised, though it must be emphasised that with careful management of the process, the results can be perfectly acceptable, if not ideal. Making film copies is expensive, though, and these then have to be stored in the right conditions, otherwise the exercise is pointless. Our successors will not thank us if we leave them a legacy of indifferent-quality copies, slowly degrading in poor storage.

Many archives are coming round to the view that the

third is the best of these options. The originals are retained in conditions which will greatly extend their life, and a high-quality digitisation programme, starting with the most vulnerable films, is embarked upon. A significant by-product of this belt-and-braces approach, and one which may justify the whole policy in the eyes of whoever is funding the archive, is the ease with which access versions of the highest quality can be generated as part of the digitisation. The uncertainty surrounding the reliability of digital preservation is mitigated by the fact that the original film remains the ultimate backstop in the case of failure. There is every expectation that our successors will thank us if we manage to pursue this policy effectively, although in the short term we may struggle to manage the unwieldy digital files.

What if the archive simply cannot afford physical storage to the required standard or if the bulk of the collection has already degraded beyond the salvation of any type of storage? Might it be justifiable to take the fourth option of leaving the films where they are, and staking everything on digital preservation? Given the relative immaturity of digital film preservation, it would still be highly advisable to retain the films as a backup for as long as they are viable, in the hope that truly secure and affordable digital preservation becomes a reality before the films have gone too far. At present, the risk of a catastrophic loss of digital data is all too real for any responsible archive to consider actively destroying the original films after copying. Film archivists might be uncomfortable with this fourth option, but in very real situations archives around the world are dealing with advanced degradation of large parts of their collections, and pursuing a less compromised approach may lead directly to serious loss.

There is one option which will surely guarantee the scorn of our successors, and that is doing nothing. There may be a few Iron Pillars in the collection which through some lucky circumstances happen to survive complete neglect, but the life expectancy of most films unprotected from the rigours of the environment is brief, and in the wrong climate with the wrong films, doing nothing is the equivalent of wilful destruction. In such circumstances, archives have sometimes been forced to take urgent steps, such as copying films on to videotape, in order to save at least something of their collection. Inevitably they now face the consequences of having pinned their hopes on such an ephemeral medium as video. But if we are truly on the brink of an age when digital scanning is cheap and data can be stored reliably, then it will become possible to carry out such urgent interventions with very little compromise in quality. A rescue-by-digitisation programme may require careful timing: the sooner it is done, the less the originals will have degraded and the lower the risk of losing them outright; on the other hand, the more time the technology has to evolve, the better will be the quality of the digital version and the easier (and cheaper) it will be to manage the digital files.

How the preserved films will be presented to an audience in the future is a different matter entirely. Unless we can find a way of preserving an original unfaded show print, or at least a modern copy carefully matched to that original, it may be difficult for our successors to say exactly how the film originally looked and sounded. Is it enough to hand down to them the copies we have preserved with no instructions as to how to generate a presentation copy? Will they understand enough about the original technology to get anywhere close? Will there even be an audience for this ancient technology, with its limited colour palette and slow frame rate, outside of some future 20th-century-themed visitor attraction? None of this will matter if the films haven't survived in the first place, and for too many archives, time is running out. Film is not forever, and if finding a way to preserve the content requires us to make compromises, we must fully understand what these entail. Above all, we cannot sit back and allow the material entrusted to us to decay before our eyes.

David Walsh is the Head of Digital Collections at the Imperial War Museum, London and Head of the Technical Commission of the International Federation of Film Archives (FIAF).

RESTORATION: A FILM HISTORIAN'S POINT OF VIEW

PETER BAGROV

Sergei Eisenstein's *Ivan the Terrible, Part 1* (1944) **Image:** Artkino Pictures Inc. / Photofest

I won't even try to come up with any formulas, or provide any technical details. I only want to give some examples of how all sorts of historical data—however insignificant they may seem—can help restore a film. There is only one aspect of film restoration I am referring to in this little essay, but that aspect is an essential one: textology.

Gosfilmofond, the Russian state film archive, holds one of the largest and most valuable film collections in the world. The core of this collection consists of fiction and animation films made in Russia and the Soviet republics: practically everything that has survived can be found at Gosfilmofond. From the late 1940s every film company (and the Soviet film industry, I might remind you, was entirely state-run) was obliged to hand in a cluster of materials for each motion picture: camera negatives, fine grain and master positive prints. It was a legal deposit, a system we still have in Russia.

Gosfilmofond is known not only for preserving Russian and Soviet national film heritage, but also for its unique collection of world cinema from the 1900s to the 1940s. The sources of this collection are worth mentioning. A significant number of these films arrived in 1945 from the Reichsfilmarchiv as a 'war trophy', which apart from German pictures contained a significant amount of films from France, USA and several other countries. Another important part of Gosfilmofond's foreign collection con-sists of Russian distribution prints of foreign films from the silent era.

The Soviet Union happened to be one of the first countries in the world to do preservation work on a large scale. Being aware of all the dangers of storing nitrates, Gosfilmofond decided to transfer everything onto safety film as early as the 1960s. This work was successfully completed by the end of the 1970s. Thereafter, only some unidentified films remained on nitrate; everything else was preserved. But the flip side of the coin was that after this preservation work, Gosfilmofond immediately disposed of the nitrate positives. Negatives were kept, since they were consid-ered to be the originals, but positives, it was argued, were not unique and therefore, need not be preserved. As the safety copies had no tinting and toning, the only record of the film's look was lost; very few archivists were con-cerned with those issues back then. As a result, several generations of Russian scholars were raised with a very dim notion of colour in silent cinema (to mention just one of the negative side-effects).

Now comes the time to correct the mistakes of the past. But what sources should we use for restoration? The answer: any sources we find useful! Let's consider a few examples.

Sergei Eisenstein's *Ivan the Terrible* (1944-45) is a black-and-white film with two beautiful colour sequences. One of them, an orgy of the drunken *oprichniki* (czar's guards), precedes the powerful black-and-white climax of the film, the murder scene in the cathedral. Between these two sequences there is a tiny scene in the palace court, which is disturbing and distracting in spite of its sophisticated camerawork, because of an unexpected shift from colour to very modest black and white. And yet, this passage could be essential and harmonious, if it were treated properly. For in the original prints, it had a blue tint, providing the perfect transition from colour to expressionist black and white. We have no studio records, no marks on the negative to suggest this, but we do have a reference from Yakov Butovskii's book on the cameraman Andrei Moskvin. Butovskii was not only a thorough film scholar, but an accurate memoirist as well. He saw the nitrate print as a student in 1946, and re-watched it in the 1960s. Being aware of the significance of tinting in this masterpiece of camerawork, he described it carefully[1]. These memoirs of a film historian would be invaluable for an authentic restoration of the film.

Another thing a restorer needs to keep in mind is the his-tory of censorship. Russian film history provides plenty of data on this. A perfect example was discovered recently by Artyom Sopin, one of the leading young film historians in Russia. One of Gosfilmofond's future restorations is the revolutionary drama *Vyborgskaya Storona* (The Vyborg Side, 1938) by Grigoriy Kozintsev and Leonid Trauberg. There are no issues of tinting and toning with this film: it is perfectly black and white, and we have the camera neg-ative too. What more could a restorer wish for? But there is a problem... the film has been released several times. It was first released in 1938. Then during the 'Thaw', an anti-Stalinist era, scenes with Stalin were excised twice (in 1954 and 1957). Whatever was left of Stalin was removed for a major re-release in 1962: not only were all the remaining scenes with Stalin cut out, so were all the shots with his portraits on the walls; any dialogue which mentioned Stalin's name was re-dubbed.

Gosfilmofond holds materials for all these versions. The remains of the camera negative can be found in the 1962

[1]Butovskii, Yakov, 2012. *Andrei Moskvin, kinooperator*. Moscow: Eizenshtein-tsentr. p. 207-209

version. Most of the excerpts with Stalin are stored as supplementary material for the 1938 version (though the 'body' of this holding is in fact a truncated dupe neg). But there is another problem: some of these excerpts lack a soundtrack. Fortunately one of the scenes with Stalin was included in a propaganda short made during World War II, *Vstrecha s Maksimom* (Meeting with Maxim, 1941). This short was never released afterwards—so nobody touched the print.

The puzzle could be put together, as you can see, by combining elements from several prints. But in order to do that a restorer has to study the censorship story scrupulously.

One more example, a case that is at the same time inspiring and hopeless. In 1962 Marlen Khutsiev made *Zastava Ilyicha*, a masterpiece of the Russian 'New Wave' that some historians consider to be the best Soviet film of the 1960s. It was banned immediately, causing a huge stir among the intellectuals. However, the film was not shelved completely and Khutsiev was given the opportunity to re-edit it himself. He had to cut out some of the sequences that were dear to him, and replace some of the actors, as well as re-write the risky dialogues. It took him more than two years, but he used the opportunity to correct some of the technical and artistic mistakes of the film to make it tenser, harsher, and more visually challenging. This version was released in 1965 as *Mne dvadtsat let* (I am Twenty) and was a great success. A quarter of a century later Khutsiev was finally permitted to release the original version. Eager to do this, he was at the same time sorry to sacrifice some of his new solutions. So he combined the two versions and made a third one, claiming quite simple-heartedly that he was merely restoring the original. This new version made quite a splash during the Perestroika.

So what we have now are three versions: each is historically significant, each is artistically powerful. Which one should be restored? Which one should be screened? I believe a restorer has to become an expert in film history, in political history, even in psychology to make a more or less circumspect decision. I wouldn't take the liberty of making a choice—at least not yet.

Another thing a restorer has to be aware of is the practice of making multiple negatives. For decades, it was common in many countries to shoot a film with two cameras and subsequently edit two negatives, one for domestic release, and the other for foreign distribution. Russia knew three periods of 'double negatives'. The first one was 1908-1914 when Pathé and Gaumont were the lead-

ing production companies in the country. A typical mistake was made by Gosfilmofond during the restoration of *L'Khaim* (1910), the first Russian film with a Jewish theme. Gosfilmofond holds two prints of the film: a tinted nitrate and a safety print. The former lacks several sequences and is decomposing badly; the latter, though complete, has neither tinting nor intertitles. During the restoration the missing parts of the nitrate were replaced with corresponding ones from the safety print. And only when the work was almost finished did the restorers realise that the two prints originated from different negatives. Such a restoration (which should by rights be called a reconstruction) is permissible if no other sources are available, but the liberties taken by the restorer should be described clearly in the credits.

The second period of 'double negatives' in Russia was in the latter half of the 1920s. We don't have any statistics at the moment, but the existence of two negatives is mentioned in several archival documents referring to the Leningrad Sovkino film factory, and Gosfilmofond owns double negatives for several blockbusters made in Moscow, at the Mezhrabpomfilm studios. The archive used to have many more in the period from the late 1940s to the early 1950s, but most of these prints did not survive; archivists of the past were concerned with preserving the film *per se*, not taking into account the issue of versions. That is why it is now vitally important to compare prints of Soviet silents in various archives: they might come from different negatives.

The third and last major period of double negatives was from 1946 to 1952 (though some occur as late as 1958). We do not have the exact records, but it seems that this was the norm for colour films. Fortunately, Gosfilmofond has preserved most of them. I am going to present just one case study, perhaps the most complicated one.

Igor Savchenko's *Taras Shevchenko* (1950), the story of Ukraine's greatest poet, was meant to be one of many post-war Stalinist biopics about the dominating role of Russian culture over the cultures of the Soviet republics. The message is obvious, and yet many scenes of this film demonstrate an entirely different tendency—to depict the tragedy of an artist under tyranny (Czarist Russia in Shevchenko's case or, metaphorically, Stalinist Soviet Union in the case of Savchenko). Savchenko died of a heart attack on December 14, 1950, the very day his film was accepted by the big Artistic Council of the Central Committee of the Communist Party. Accepted by the Artistic Council, but not by the head of the country: some changes still had to be made on Stalin's personal orders.

Taras Shevchenko: In 1950 with actress Ada Voitsik (above) and the 1951 version with Natalia Uzhviy (below). **Courtesy**: Gosfilmofond

Taras Shevchenko was reshot partially by Savchenko's pupils Aleksandr Alov, Vladimir Naumov and Grigori Melik-Avakian, and released a year later in December 1951. It received the highest state award, the Stalin Prize.

What Gosfilmofond has are three different versions: not only the two camera negatives of the 'final' version, but also a positive print of Savchenko's original version preserved only in black and white. The lack of colour has always stopped archivists and film scholars from considering Savchenko's original as the essential version, for *Taras Shevchenko* is known for its beautiful colour cinematography. In order to justify the common preference for re-edited versions, historians usually turn to memoirs, which is always a risky step. The only living member of

the crew, Vladimir Naumov (who later became an established director himself) told the story many times and recorded it in his memoirs. One of the major changes that had to be made after Savchenko's death was the addition of a pathetic scene of Shevchenko's meeting with his sister Yaryna (he is a former serf who has been set free, but she is still a serf). At a meeting with Savchenko's young pupils, Ivan Bolshakov, the Cinema Minister, passed on Stalin's question, "Where's Yaryna?," meaning that Yaryna should be mentioned in the film. Alov, Naumov and Melik-Avakian were commissioned to shoot the new scene with Ukraine's leading theatrical actress Natalia Uzhviy[2].

All of this would seem quite simple, if only we didn't have Savchenko's original version. Because there she is, Yaryna, in a long and impressive scene—only here she is played by another actress, Ada Voitsik.

Voitsik led a very discreet life, rarely gave interviews, and never wrote her memoirs, so there was no chance of getting her point of view. Uzhviy, on the other hand, was active until her late eighties and welcomed publicity. She had one small book of memoirs dedicated entirely to her film work. Surely, since she did not make that many films, there would be something in it about Yaryna. And indeed, there it was, Uzhviy pathetically describing... how Savchenko himself worked with her[3]. According to archival documents, however, Savchenko worked only with Voitsik, and had never had any time to reshoot her scenes. In fact, he died before Stalin watched his film and decided to cast Uzhviy[4].

We should be grateful to memoirists in the case of *Ivan the Terrible*. But in the case of *Taras Shevchenko*, they are not to be trusted. Neither the dead ones, nor the living.

So once again: what should be our reference for a restoration? The answer is: anything we can find. Technologies advance, film restoration becomes more and more academic, and yet, there is no way to avoid film history. And exciting though it is, film history remains, in the end, a terribly subjective business.

Peter Bagrov is a widely published writer and film historian. He has lectured on the history of Russian cinema and is currently Senior Curator of the Russian state film archive Gosfilmofond.

[2] Naumov, Vladimir; Belokhvostikova, Natalia, 2000. *V kadre*. Moscow: Tsentrpoligraf. p. 29-30.
[3] Uzhviy, Natalia, 1977. *Filmy, druzia, gody*. Moscow: BPSK. p. 43-44
[4] Sopin, Artyom, 2015. 'Sovetskie filmy o Tarase Shevchenko.' In *Shevchenkiana v raznykh vidakh iskusstva*. Moscow: RGALI (forthcoming).

FILM PRESERVATION AROUND THE WORLD

The problems that beset film preservation in India are familiar to archivists around the world: limited budgets and resources, a general lack of awareness and a reluctance among administrators to acknowledge film as an integral part of a nation's cultural heritage. Here is a look at the innovative solutions that international film archives have found for these problems, from discovering ways to attract younger audiences, to persuading governments to invest in digitisation programmes.

Restoration of *Camera Buff*, directed by Krzysztof Kieślowski, 1979, Rights: Studio Filmowe TOR

THE HITCHCOCK 9

Robin Baker, head curator, BFI National Archive, on how the BFI took Hitchcock's silent films to new audiences around the world. A case study in fundraising, building awareness of restoration, and the marketing of restored classics.

I was 10 years old when I had my first encounter with Britain's greatest, most famous and most recognisable filmmaker. It was the 1970s and I was allowed to stay up late to watch *The Birds* (1963) on my family's black and white portable television. I was riveted and terrified in equal measure. I was also hooked.

I devoured *Rear Window* (1954) and *The Man Who Knew Too Much* (1956) when they appeared on TV and, like many people, assumed that Hitchcock's talent magically appeared when he landed in the United States to direct *Rebecca* (1940). But the reality is that some of his most important work was made in Britain in the 1920s and 30s.

Between 1925 and 1929 Hitchcock shot ten silent films in Britain and Germany. One of these, *The Mountain Eagle* (1927), no longer exists—part of the 80% of British silent cinema that was 'lost', destroyed, decomposed or discarded before the advent of film archives. However, the nine surviving silent films are central to the understanding of his work. Only two of these films, *The Lodger* (1927) and *Blackmail* (1929), conform to what we would recognise as the classic Hitchcock thriller. But all of them are imbibed with elements we'd now call 'Hitchcockian'— whether it's his trademark use of dark humour, his many obsessions that range from blonde women to food, or his brilliant construction of imaginative set-pieces or shots. It was in the 1920s that he conceived, tried out and refined the visual storytelling ideas that he would revisit and rework in film after film. Making silent films taught Hitchcock how to use images, not words, to tell his stories—what Hitchcock called 'pure cinema', a skill he learned in part from German and Russian cinema. The young Hitch was not only a great artist, but by the end of the decade he was the most successful and famous director working in Britain.

Despite the quality of this work, trying to see one of Hitchcock's silent films when I was growing up was impossible. Even in the DVD and online age they existed only in badly damaged and incomplete versions with musical soundtracks that didn't exactly enhance the viewing experience. Indeed, for decades Hitchcock's first film, *The Pleasure Garden* (1926), only existed in copies that were missing 20 minutes from the original running time. It's no more acceptable or enjoyable than, for example, trying to read Dickens' first novel, *The Pickwick Papers*, if 150 pages had been excised from your copy.

The restoration of Hitchcock's silent films—or 'the Hitchcock 9' as we started to call them—was a long-held ambition of the BFI National Archive. However, we knew that it would be both complex and expensive. Given the extent of the damage to materials, it was an undertaking that was not even feasible until the advent of the digital restoration technologies that enable us to significantly transform the quality of the image.

By committing ourselves to such a major undertaking we needed to be 100% clear why we were doing it. With a project that was going to cost in excess of £1,000,000 it was not acceptable simply to restore the films, screen them at a handful of festivals to devotees of silent cinema, and then return them to a climate-controlled shelf at the archive. We needed to ensure that they reached new audiences and that we could transform understanding and awareness of Hitchcock's early work.

Changing understanding of Hitchcock's early work was central to the project from the outset. Our proposition to audiences was this: if you don't know the silents, you don't know Hitchcock. But the only way to achieve this was to present the films in a way that made them desirable to audiences who had not previously watched a silent film. The presentation of the restorations would be something that was wholly integral to the restoration project and planned from the outset—not just a last minute add-on. If we were to bring about change we needed to be ambitious. In a world of limited budgets it was going to be was something of a challenge. However, with the announcement that London would host the 2012 Olympic Games—and the associated Cultural Olympiad, Festival 2012—we knew that we would have an extraordinary launchpad for the project when the eyes of the world would be on Britain.

A key part of the ambition was in place, but the money wasn't. Each year the BFI contributes an amount from its grant-in-aid funding from the UK government towards the restoration of a handful of British films. We knew

Screening of *Blackmail* (1929) at the British Museum. **Image:** BFI

Nitin Sawhney conducting his new score for *The Lodger* (1927). **Image:** BFI

that this funding alone would only cover a fraction of the costs of our plans, so we required a major fundraising initiative to achieve the £1,000,000+ price tag for restoring the films and mounting the events. An international fundraising campaign—'Rescue the Hitchcock 9'—was launched in 2010 that reached out not only to the trusts, foundations and individuals who already generously supported the BFI's work, but to Hitchcock fans across the world. A dedicated page on the BFI's website made it easy for anyone to donate. No amount was too small—or too large. Between them, the smaller donations made a significant contribution towards achieving our targets. They also enabled many people to have a sense of possession on the project. We even made it clear how many frames of film each donation would enable us to restore. Donations came in from all over the globe—from the United States to India to South Korea to Australia—underlining how much people saw Hitchcock's work as world heritage. It was not just the money that was important: the fundraising campaign helped to underline awareness of the fragility of film as a medium and that its need for restoration is every bit as essential as work that might be undertaken on the Mona Lisa or the Taj Mahal. Transforming understanding about the need for film preservation and restoration was another cornerstone of the project, and this was a story that we would tell through online films and blogs, programme notes and the media.

Bringing new music to the films was also key. None of the original scores for Hitchcock's silent films survive, so we had the freedom to imagine different musical styles and approaches that might work with them and with new audiences. In selecting and commissioning a diverse range of British composers, we had our eye on the different audiences that each would bring to the project and the stories that we would be able to tell. Composers selected ranged from Nitin Sawhney, who created a head-

ily romantic and thrilling full orchestral score for *The Lodger*, to saxophonist Soweto Kinch, who brought the energy and dynamism of 21st century jazz to Hitchcock's Jazz Age film, *The Ring* (1927).

The shaping of the presentation of each of the films would be paramount if we were to attract a substantial new audience and ensure that they had a great time. We launched the project with three performances of *The Pleasure Garden* with a brilliantly innovative score for 13-piece ensemble by young composer Daniel Patrick Cohen. It was his first film composition—quite appropriate for Hitchcock's first film. Performances took place at Wilton's Music Hall, the world's oldest surviving music hall and one of London's most atmospheric buildings. The unique offer guaranteed an almost instant sell-out and the perfect launch for the project. A range of very different locations and approaches followed, but the most resonant took place outside the British Museum. The great Hitchcockian set-piece near the end of his final silent, *Blackmail*, takes place at the British Museum, so the 2000-strong audience were able to watch the movie at the very location that Hitch shot it 83 years previously.

Although screenings were planned in cinemas across the UK later in the summer, we worked to ensure that audiences outside London could enjoy the 'live' aspect of three of the events. The premiere of the restoration of *The Lodger* at the 2000-seat Barbican Hall with Nitin Sawhney conducting the London Symphony Orchestra was simultaneously broadcast to 20 cinemas around Britain. And the premieres of *The Ring* and *Champagne* (1928) were broadcast live online complete with interviews with the composers.

To ensure that new audiences were not left to watch the films without wider context, each film screening was introduced alongside a short film that showed the specific challenges that the team faced with each restoration. Audiences were also given programme notes, supplying them with more background information. Additionally, a new online resource and book—*The 39 Steps to Hitchcock*—-were launched, each of which placed Hitch's British work at the heart of the wider story of his life and career.

The BFI's marketing team created a strong brand for the project, featuring an image of Hitch himself that has subsequently been used internationally. This included the creation of Hitchcock masks—an idea that ensured that thousands of people tweeted images of themselves looking like the master of suspense and thereby building awareness of the project.

The restorations were also central to the BFI's complete retrospective of Hitchcock's work that also took place during the summer of 2012. However, here Hitchcock's silent films were the stars of the show, rather than the more obvious *Vertigo, North by Northwest* or *Psycho*. We had something new to say about Hitchcock, and press and audiences loved it.

Given the amount of attention generated by the Festival 2012 events, the Hitchcock 9 soon began their trip across the world, appearing to date in over 30 countries. Highlights have included 7000 people on Rio de Janeiro's Copacabana beach watching *The Pleasure Garden*; the sell-out screenings and ecstatic audiences at the Shanghai International Film Festival and, best of all, the crowd of 25,000 people who watched and applauded *Blackmail* on Odessa's Potemkin Steps right in the middle of the crisis in Ukraine during the summer of 2014. These performances would not have been possible without the collaboration of the British Council who transformed our ability to screen the film internationally.

It's been hugely rewarding to share these films with over 250,000 people across the globe and demonstrate that they are part of world heritage, not just British heritage. And as they continue their journey it's reassuring to know that they are fully preserved in the BFI's new Master Film Store in Warwickshire where they are kept very cold and very dry. This will add hundreds of years to their life expectancy, ensuring that they are safe for future generations. I hope that means that Hitchcock's silent films will never need to be restored again.

THE KinoRP PROJECT

Maciej Molewski on a pioneering Polish digital restoration project which brought the private and public sectors together to rescue Poland's cinematic heritage from decades of neglect.

In the mid-fifties, a new style of filmmaking began in Poland, often referred to as the Polish film school. The nucleus of this was a young generation of filmmakers—directors, cinematographers, actors—who tried to bring their own forms of expression to cinema, and touch upon matters important to the new generation. By distancing themselves from classic forms and the aesthetic of socialist realism, filmmakers such as Andrzej Wajda, Jerzy Kawalerowicz, Wojciech Jerzy Has, Janusz Morgenstern and Tadeusz Konwicki created a new trend in Polish cinema that made it renowned throughout the world. Though they lived and worked under a Communist regime with omnipresent censorship, they managed to make films which were not only independent of socialist doctrine, but even critical of it, by taking recourse to a language of images.

Meanwhile, the regime continued to view cinema as an important tool of propaganda, and reserved the right to decide each film's fate, right from the script approval stage to the distribution of the films and the preservation of their prints. Because Polish cinema was poorly funded, films were made with the use of low-quality equipment. On top of that, filmmakers considered 'difficult' by the regime suffered constant obstacles, even repression. As a result, many talented filmmakers such as Roman Polański, Jerzy Skolimowski, Krzysztof Kieślowski and Andrzej Żuławski left the country. For those who didn't leave, making films meant a relentless fight for camera film, equipment, number of shooting days, almost everything. Many acclaimed films were completed in these appalling conditions, including such classics as *Kanal* directed by Andrzej Wajda, *Hourglass Sanatorium* by

The restoration of *Night Train*, directed
by Jerzy Kawalerowicz, 1959
Rights: Studio Filmowe KADR

Wojciech Jerzy Has, *Pharaoh* by Jerzy Kawalerowicz and *Last Day of Summer* by Tadeusz Konwicki. For these filmmakers international recognition was often their salvation from the might of the regime.

Unfortunately this did not save their films. In a way, the regime succeeded: its strict control over the entire film industry, which lasted for decades, resulted in bringing the films it archived to the verge of extinction. Poland, like all the Eastern Bloc countries, followed the Cold War strategy of the Soviets in criticizing everything that was connected to the western world, including policies of archiving and the preservation of film stock. It implemented and followed its own rules instead. The consequent lack of proper standards resulted in the degradation of films, on a much larger scale than in the Western world.

Even after 1989 when the regime ended, the condition of our archives was not recognised as an important matter. The situation didn't change until the turn of the new millennium when Grzegorz Molewski (later founder of the KinoRP project) launched the first television channel dedicated to Polish cinema, and thus created the impetus to re-examine the condition of Polish film heritage.

The situation was grave. There was no reliable information on the location of film copies and their condition. As a result, the distribution of films was chaotic: different versions of the same film were in circulation simultaneously, and in other cases there were no copies at all. The level of degradation was high; the picture and the sound, whatever was left of them, had nothing to do with the

original films themselves. Unstable images, flickering, strange colouration or lack of contrast, spliced or lost fragments, scratches, mould and geometrical distortions were the catastrophic consequences of decades of disrespectful treatment. "We realised that practically nobody in Poland knew the masterpieces of Polish cinema from watching films, only from their synopses. The fact that *Kanal* or *Ashes and Diamonds* were good films was known from the literature. But when we were watching these films we were seeing only decayed images and strange versions," recalls Grzegorz Molewski. Even though his immediate concern was finding good copies for the television channel, he soon realised that the repercussions could be far worse: the lack of good copies could result in a decrease of interest in Polish cinema, and damage its cultural value.

In those days, very few people in Poland were aware of the situation. Although some efforts were made towards correcting damaged copies, mainly for the purpose of DVD releases, the lack of proper technology and an intelligent approach often caused more harm than good.

The change came in 2006. As a part of a series of films directed by Wojciech Jerzy Has and released by Grzegorz Molewski, *Hourglass Sanatorium* was to undergo colour correction under the supervision of the original cinematographer, Witold Sobociński (known for such films as *Hands Up* by Jerzy Skolimowski and *Frantic* by Roman Polański). He convinced Molewski to upgrade the quality of film mastering from Standard Definition (SD) to High Definition (HD) resolution. Soon after the scanning of the film, however, everyone realised that the higher resolution made the damage to the picture more noticeable and mere colour correction wouldn't be enough: in order to deliver better quality, the work would require investing in digital restoration equipment.

This was done, and the restoration completed. There was a noticeable lack of interest from the filmmaking community (the screening of *Hourglass Sanatorium* drew only seven people) but Grzegorz Molewski persevered and started restoring *Night Train* by Jerzy Kawalerowicz, filmmaker and founder of the KADR Film Studio. The decision was made that the end result of the restoration process must be a professional digital cinema copy (DCP) in 2K resolution. The digital image restoration was co-financed by Grzegorz Molewski's company and KADR Film Studio. As previously, a special screening of the restored film was planned. Grzegorz Molewski reminisces, "At the screening of the newly restored *Night Train* many people came, including filmmakers, and at last it seemed that people understood. I remember the conversation after the screening with a famous Polish cinematographer, who came to me and asked where we had obtained such an immaculate print. He couldn't believe that the film was shown from a digital copy. Then I understood that for filmmakers, 'digital copy' brought to mind something crude, since up to that moment, they had only seen low-quality digital images, blurred with washed-out colours." This was the beginning of the breakthrough: the support of the filmmakers' community for the results of digital restoration opened the doors for the KinoRP project.

After the success of the *Night Train* screening, work started on further films from the KADR Film Studio. Based on the newly formed model of co-financing, the next films to be restored were Andrzej Wajda's *Ashes and Diamonds* and Jerzy Kawalerowicz's *Austeria*. Simultaneously a standardised model of functionality and rules of financing was being developed. The objective was not the digitisation and digital restoration itself, but the survival of our film heritage through the distribution of high-quality digital copies of films for cinemas, television, DVD, Blu-ray and internet viewing. It required the exploration of new areas of competence, including archiving and universal distribution of films to the mainstream.

In those days there weren't any systematic routines or proven solutions in place for this, even in other countries. Given the number of Polish films, it was clear that nobody could take on such a task alone. So Grzegorz Molewski worked out an approach based on the co-operation of a network of public institutions, film studios, filmmakers and technological companies. He believed that co-opera-

tion between all the parties would open up opportunities to restore larger quantities of our films. The problem of financing remained. Public institutions hadn't developed effective instruments of financial support yet and subsequent restorations were still co-financed by Grzegorz Molewski with the film studios.

The growing number of digitally restored films, as well as the dialogue initiated by film studios with film institutions and the Ministry of Culture and National Heritage, brought in the expected results in 2010. The European Union (EU) recognised the role of digitisation in preserving European film heritage, leading to the creation of programme co-financing for the preservation of the film heritage of member nations. Thanks to the newly available funds, the Ministry of Culture and National Heritage provided in its 2010-2015 budget for the digitisation as well as the digital restoration of classic Polish cinema. The first institution which supported these processes was the Polish Film Institute, and soon after another financial programme based on EU funds and coordinated by the National Audiovisual Institute, was started.

But public support didn't sort out all of the problems, because it didn't cover more than 70% of the full costs of the restoration. Grzegorz Molewski therefore continued to co-finance restorations for another two years. A year later the KinoRP project found a patron of digital restoration, PKO Bank Polski, the largest bank in Poland. Thanks to its continuous support, twenty more films could be restored.

Today, the KinoRP Project continues with its aim of saving the heritage of Polish cinematic art by digitally restoring its masterpieces to produce digital copies of the highest quality. It brings classical Polish movies to audiences everywhere, whether they are watching in the theatres or at home, introducing the younger generation to the best of the country's cinema. All the digital restoration takes place with the personal participation of the original authors: the directors and the cinematographers, who supervise the remastering from an artistic point of view.

The project is carried out in cooperation with the Polish Film Institute, the National Audiovisual Institute and the Polish Filmmakers Association, as well as the KADR, Tor and Zebra film studios. The co-operation of public institutions and the private sector has resulted in an increase in the number of digitally restored films. Despite this obvious success, several issues have not yet been resolved. In 2010, under the auspices of UNESCO and with the co-operation of the Ministry of Culture and National Heritage, a seminar was held which focussed on the key concerns of Polish classical cinema, highlighting such aspects as

- the lack of a reliable registry of Polish archives, including even the basic knowledge of the state of copies of our films,
- the need for steadfast procedures in digital restoration,
- the need for the regulation of standards in the film selection process and policies regarding preservation, archiving and indexing of restored films.

Despite a general atmosphere of understanding, most of the analysed problems and demands have still not been solved. Since 2010, the KinoRP project has organised further seminars and workshops in Poland addressing the problems and challenges of the digital era. As the result, there has been a significant growth in consciousness which has helped shaped the rules for saving Polish film heritage. Since the first film restored under the KinoRP project, nearly 250 films (including full feature films, documentaries and animations) have been completely restored and returned to the open market thanks to the support of a network of filmmakers such as Andrzej Wajda, Krzysztof Zanussi, Wojciech Marczewski; cinematographers Witold Sobociński, Jerzy Wójcik, Grzegorz Kędzierski; sound directors Wiesława Dembińska, Michał Żarnecki, Marek Wronko; and the participation of technologists such as Jędrzej Sabliński from DI Factory, Wojciech Janio from Fixafilm, Dariusz Jankowski from TPS, Tomasz Dukszta from Soundplace, Radosław Skłodowski from SSD, Wojciech Kabarowski from The Chimney, Poland and many more.

ASIAN FILM ARCHIVES

Film archives across Asia have had to contend with many of the same issues faced in India, such as bureaucratic apathy and insufficient funding. Wenchi Lin of the Taiwan Film Institute and Chalida Uabumrungjit of the Thai Film Archive describe how their respective institutions have tackled the many challenges facing Asian film archives today.

TAIWAN FILM INSTITUTE

Before 1978, Taiwan did not have any organisation responsible for collecting, restoring, preserving and researching films. Most films made during the 1930s and 40s had been damaged or lost, as were most Taiwan films made in the 50s and 60s by companies other than the three studios owned by the government. The record for films made in the decades up to the 1980s was scarcely better. Many films were destroyed due to poor management or because movie companies had shut down, making it very difficult to research the history of Taiwanese movies.

The Chinese Taipei Film Archive (CTFA) was set up to conserve the country's film heritage, and after thirty-four years of history, upgraded in 2014 to become the Taiwan Film Institute (TFI), a foundation set up by the Ministry of Culture. With close to 15,000 Taiwan or Chinese film titles in its collection, the Institute has a mission to preserve Taiwan cinema, and also to promote Taiwan film and documentary through two new departments, the Taiwan International Documentary Festival Office and the Overseas Market Department.

Despite TFI's expansion, film archival work remains our core mission. Out of 1800 films shot in Taiwanese, only around 200 still exist. Given this dire situation, it was not difficult to convince the government that the nation's film treasures needed to be preserved for the sake of future generations. Although the annual budget of TFI is small, the Ministry of Culture helps with funding for work such as rescuing endangered films, duplicating prints in bad condition, and digitally restoring important films from the collection. Among the first batch of eight titles restored in 2013 was King Hu's *Dragon Inn*, which was selected by Cannes to be screened in its classics section in 2014.

Over the years, TFI/CTFA has invited government officials and legislators to visit the storage vaults to observe their not-so-desirable condition, which is a result of insufficient funding. We tried to make them understand that this precious cultural heritage was fragile and needed to be kept carefully at a low temperature with humidity control. The former Minister of Culture Ms. Long Ying-tai

The restoration of King Hu's classic
Dragon Inn (1967)
Courtesy: Taiwan Film Institute

added about 300,000 US dollars to our annual budget after her visit, and in fact, was responsible for upgrading the CTFA to the TFI, as a strategic move designed to make it easier to ask for more funding.

In the past, TFI/CTFA has tried to raise money by offering honorary membership to donors. The public's response to that was not enthusiastic, so we decided to be more aggressive in our fund-raising. We asked the Minister of Culture to hold a press conference to call for support for the preservation of Taiwan's film heritage in response to UNESCO's call for a World Day for Audiovisual Heritage. We invited the highly respected veteran director Lee Hsing, as well as movie stars Bridget Lin and Shi Jun to be the 'Guardian Angels' of Taiwan's old films. We also raised funds by screening *Dragon Inn* in fifty theatres with the support of the theatre owners. The events were a success as they received a significant amount of media coverage and made people aware of the importance of film preservation.

Since our budget for film restoration is limited, TFI actively seeks donations from individuals and corporations. Films on the to-be-restored waiting list are put in three categories in order to approach different target groups for financial support: classics renowned for their aesthetic achievement; films starring famous actors or actresses; and classics made in Taiwanese. Among the films restored in 2014, *A Touch of Zen* (1970) by King Hu, for example, is a masterpiece of Taiwan cinema. Its restoration was solely sponsored by its leading actress Hsu Feng, who is also a successful producer and business woman. *Love in Chilly Spring* (1979) is the first film the superstar singer Feng Feifei starred in. We invited Feng's fan clubs to participate in the restoration project and started a call for donations on the internet. We prepared different gifts for the donors, such as memorial crystal stands, booklets, and Blu-ray DVDs, to encourage them to donate. The money needed for the restoration was raised in two months, in time for the premiere screening on Feng's birthday.

Another popular film restored is *The Young Ones* (1973), which stars another superstar actress, Chen Chen. After the restoration was done, we invited Chen Chen to the press conference and premiere screening at Golden Horse Film Festival. Chen Chen was happy to see the beautifully restored film and donated 36,000 dollars to our institute to show her gratitude.

TFI has recently begun to work with one of the largest banks in Taiwan. We will launch an annual event for the bank's credit card holders to support film preservation and restoration by donating the card's reward points to TFI. Hopefully, the bank will also sponsor the organisation of a film festival of digitally restored classics of Taiwan and World cinema, to convey the importance of film preservation to the public. If successful, this would be an annual event to raise funds to improve the TFI's vault facility and restore more films.

Restored films can generate income when their rights are resold to international markets. When they are re-released in local theatres, there is the income from ticket sales and the sale of related souvenirs and products. To encourage rights-holders to work with TFI to restore their films, TFI not only pays for the restoration, but also yields 20% to 30% of the total income generated. So far this has been a successful strategy. With its annual funding from the government, TFI now plans to purchase a scanner and scan the films on its own, besides setting up restoration workstations to restore films in-house. All this should greatly reduce the cost of restoring a film.

Dome Sukvong, founder of the Thai Film Archive.
Courtesy: Thai Film Archive

THAI FILM ARCHIVE

Looking back to when the Thai Film Archive first started in the 1980s, no one in Thailand then seemed to know or care much about film preservation. As a young researcher, Dome Sukvong, the founder of the film archive, discovered a collection of nitrate films of the Royal State Railway's Topical Film Service, dating back to the 1920s. There was no place for film preservation in the country at the time. In 1983, Dome was invited to participate in a workshop for the International Federation of Film Archives in Sweden. He was inspired by what he learned there. During his visit, he got to know about newsreel footage of King Rama V's visit to Stockholm in 1897, which proved to be one of the earliest film records of the Thai nation. The footage proved to the government that film could hold tremendous historical value, and Dome received the approval to set up a section dedicated to preserving film under the Fine Arts Department. It began in 1984 with one deserted building, one table made of a wooden door, a few volunteers and no budget. Dome's team travelled around the country, collecting film and film materials—theatrical films, posters, magazines, projectors—and began building an archive. For the first 25 years, the Film Archive had to contend with the limitations of being understaffed and under-resourced, but the people who worked there always kept their films in the best condition possible.

Gaining public interest and support is the key for film preservation. The Thai Film Archive launched a campaign called Film Rescue, which sent out a van to places all over the country to collect films and other moving image media, rushing to wherever a cinema was closing down to gather whatever could be rescued. The campaign also played a part in creating awareness of film preservation.

Film preservation means a lot more than just storing and screening old films. It involves all the processes from acquisition, inspection, repair and duplication which are necessary to prolong the life of the film and bring it to a stage where it can be shown again. These days, with digital technology it is easier to revive films in a very bad condition, but all this, of course, requires time and money. At the heart of film preservation is the storage facility. Good storage, with proper temperature and climate control, is the key. It will buy time for us until we are ready to restore all the films.

In 1994 the Archive received 35 mm negatives of more than twenty titles from the Rank Laboratory in the UK. The films were produced in the period from 1955 to 1969; it was rare for Thai audiences to have the opportunity to see good quality films from this period. The Thai Film Foundation helped to fund the striking of new prints of nine of these films, which were then shown in a small film festival, Mahakam Teung Nang Thai (the Amazing Thai Film Festival) in 1995. This was the first time in many years that people had the opportunity to see new prints of Thai films in full colour. Since the prevailing impression of Thai films of the period was based on scratchy, magenta-tinged prints, this experience was both unique and striking. It really changed the perception of the importance of film preservation and restoration.

The Thai Film Archive has also taken steps towards digital restoration. It is acquiring the digital restoration workflow which will be installed in 2015. Selections will be made from the films in our collection, which consists of 1500 feature films and 9000 documentaries, for the restoration process.

Alfred Hitchcock's silent film *The Lodger* (1927) **Image**: BFI

IT IS EXTRAORDINARY THAT MEN HAVE
ENTRUSTED SO MANY IMAGES, SO MANY
AFFECTS, SO MANY CONSTRUCTIONS,
SUCH BEAUTY TO A MEDIUM SO CLOSE,
ONTOLOGICALLY, TO ITS OWN RUIN.

GEORGES DIDI-HUBERMAN
Montage, 13

INDIAN BEGINNINGS

Krishna vanquishes the serpent Kaliya, from *Gopal Krishna* (1965)

FILM PRESERVATION IN INDIA

P. K. NAIR

It is widely known that the first Indian story film, *Raja Harishchandra*, was made in 1913 by Dadasaheb Phalke. What is not known as widely is that the film perished a few years after it was made. The only surviving print of the film caught fire while it was being transported in a bullock cart from one tent cinema to another. The actual cause of the accident was not known, but it was reported that the nitrate print had already had a large number of screenings and was practically worn out, and that the accident may have happened while loading or unloading.

In 1917, when Phalke found out that the original negatives had also vanished, he re-shot the film, duplicating the original shot by shot, and taking the opportunity to insert title cards asserting his claim to be "the father of the Indian film industry" and "the great Pioneer of the East".

Like Phalke's film, many of the most important films in our history have not survived. Many have either turned to powder or have been lost in fires, through accidents or negligence. Many others were lost when silver was extracted from the nitrate films, or when cellulose film was stripped and used to prepare bangles, ladies' handbags and other curios—cottage industries that thrived parasitically off the film-making scene. According to informed sources, nearly 70% of the titles produced before 1980 have either deteriorated beyond repair or may be considered permanently lost.

There are many reasons why we are in such a dire situation today. Barring a few pioneering exceptions, most of the early films were made by businessmen, whose primary concern was making profits. Their interest in a film lasted only as long as it earned them money. Thereafter, they did not care about the whereabouts of the negatives or positive prints. Even if they did care, few had the facilities or the technical know-how to take care of highly inflammable nitrate films. As a result, many film negatives were simply allowed to perish.

Filmmakers and authorities alike were not conscious of the historical or cultural importance of cinema. Film is highly fragile material, which needs special care and attention for a longer life. However, under the British colonial regime, there were no organisations entrusted with the responsibility of treating cinema as a cultural product and ensuring its preservation for posterity. In the national consciousness, cinema always had a low level of priority: the taboos attached to the profession ensured that few people considered wasting their time in preserving films. A lack of awareness and understanding thus led to the wanton destruction of the country's film heritage.

In the years before Independence and well into the fifties, attempts at preservation were limited to stray individual efforts and a few initiatives taken by the established production companies. Under the studio system, the larger studios produced ten to fifteen films a year and had a certain stability. They built storage godowns and took care of their films as long as they were in existence. Once the studios started closing down, we saw the rise of strong independent producers like Raj Kapoor, Bimal

INDIA'S TOP TEN LOST FILMS

Bhakta Vidur (1921), directed by Kanjibhai Rathod.

Bilet Pherat / England Returned (1921), directed by N.C. Laharry.

Savkari Pash (1925), directed by Baburao Painter.

Balidan / Sacrifice (1927), directed by Naval Gandhi.

Alam Ara (1931), directed by Ardeshir M. Irani.

Sairandhri (1933), directed by V. Shantaram.

Mazdoor / The Mill (1934), directed by Mohan Bhavnani.

Seeta (1934), directed by Debaki Kumar Bose.

Khoon ka Khoon / Hamlet (1935), directed by Sohrab Modi.

Zindagi (1940), directed by P.C. Barua.

The only surviving images of
India's first talkie *Alam Ara* (1931)

Roy, Guru Dutt and others. Most of these producers ran their companies as businesses, concentrating their attention and care on successful films that continued to earn revenue, while neglecting the others.

THE BEGINNINGS OF FILM PRESERVATION IN INDIA

Officially, film preservation commenced in India with the setting up of the National Film Archive of India (NFAI), in the mid-sixties. The origin of the archive dates back to the S.K. Patil Committee Report of 1952 in which it was proposed that the government should recognise excellence in various fields of film-making and that a copy of the award-winning films should be kept in a National Film Library. The idea, then, was to preserve only award-winning films. Later, it was suggested that not only award-winning films, but all films of historical interest and others whose loss may be regretted later should be preserved for posterity. A separate media unit of the Ministry of Information and Broadcasting was entrusted with this responsibility, and the NFAI began functioning from February 1964 in Pune, Maharashtra.

Most of the Archive's collection was obtained from rights-holders, who were requested to deposit their originals, or grant permission to copy them. Very often, this was done on a verbal understanding, without any contracts signed; it was all a question of trust. There were other films where the rights were under dispute, or the

rights-owners could not be traced—in such cases, an indemnity bond was submitted, stating that the Archive would handle any claims raised by heirs or others. As a department of the central government, the Archive also managed to get all the prints that had been confiscated by the Customs or the Railways. Used prints were also sourced from foreign-film importers, foreign missions and private collectors. The Archive also exchanged prints with the national film archives of various countries and institutions such as the Museum of Modern Art. The Soviet film archive gifted twenty films, while with the British Film Institute (BFI), we were exchanging films even before the Archive was set up, trading the likes of *Sant Tukaram* (1936) for Hitchcock's films and others.

I was associated with the NFAI from its inception. At the outset, the Archive launched a hunt for the earliest films made in the country, especially those made by Dadasaheb Phalke. I got in touch with the family and managed to obtain the first reel of *Raja Harishchandra* from Phalke's daughter Mandakini. A few years later in 1969, we got to know that more material was available with Neelkanth Phalke, the pioneer's elder son who lived in Dombivili, a suburb of Mumbai. I went to visit him and immediately noticed the son's striking facial resemblance to his illustrious father, whose enlarged photograph adorned the small drawing room. After the preliminary introductions, two rusted tins were placed them before me. I examined them one by one. They contained a number of bit pieces of positive film, surprisingly in fairly good condition. Two bits were tinted blue: on close examination, I noticed the bit contained the last sequence of *Raja Harishchandra*. I was thrilled at the possibility of having the complete film, but alas, it was only the fourth reel. (The second and third reels of the film are still to be located). The tins also contained negatives of a short actuality, *Sinhasta Mela*, made by Dadasaheb in the early 1920s.

Inquiring after Phalke's other films, I was told to get in touch with the youngest Phalke son Prabhakar, who occupied the same house in Nasik where his father had spent his last years. I travelled to Nasik and reached the Phalke house early in the morning. As I went in, I was struck by the insignia of a movie camera at the entrance of the old house. Prabhakar met me with a wooden box containing stray reels and fragments from various Phalke films, a moth-eaten notebook filled with notes on shots (presumably in Dadasaheb Phalke's own hand) as well as almost all of *Kaliya Mardan* (1917). One look at the tins and I could see they had not been opened for a considerably long period. The lids were jammed and we had a difficult time opening them. A strong smell of nitrate was emanating from each tin. I noticed that some of the bits had started decomposing. In fact, a couple were already reduced to yellow pulp, and there was no alternative but to discard them there and then.

We decided that the films needed to be taken to Pune immediately. Prabhakar did not demand any compensation, but he was very particular about having a list of contents copied for his records. Formalities completed, a ride was arranged on the newspaper taxi which used to ply between Nasik and Pune for the dispatch of the daily Marathi newspapers *Sakal* and *Kesari*. The journey was long and tedious. I was constantly looking back; always conscious of the archival reels kept behind us, and every time the car bumped my heart took a jump. The transport of inflammable nitrate film was indeed risky, but we had to go through with it to save the film. We reached Pune by late evening, deposited the tins in the Archive's temporary shed, and heaved a sigh of relief.

As a footnote, I want to mention that when I was in Nasik recently for the shooting of *Celluloid Man* (2012), I discovered that the Phalke house no longer existed; a commercial complex had come up in its place. How I wish someone had saved at least one piece of our film history—the insignia with the movie camera.

Searching for prints of the other silent films made in India

was a Herculean task. It was a great adventure to visit the remote corners of the country to hunt for films. They were quite literally scattered around, turning up in such odd places as cowsheds and godowns belonging to owners of grocery shops. A few reels of Indian silent films were also found in foreign locations. Somehow, we managed to collect about nine to ten out of the 1500 silent feature films made in the country between 1913 and 1932.

Most of the family members and heirs we met in our search were happy to collaborate with us. Often, they helped us collect films, and supplied any information we needed, congratulating us for taking the pains to keep the filmmakers' memories alive. Yet there were bitter encounters as well. Sometimes, doors were shut on our faces, and we were told to get lost: "Don't ever utter the word 'film' in this house. Our father lost all the family property in making films and we have yet to recover from the loss". Then there was the time a grocery-shop owner told us, "Yes, I have a wooden box containing some old films lying in my attic. By the way, how much can you pay?" We asked to look at the box, but he would not show it despite repeated requests. "First tell me how much you are offering, and then I'll show you". I told him I needed to have a look at the material to find out whether the reels were intact or had deteriorated and turned to powder, before I could make an offer. When he refused to relent, his son took me aside to a corner and confided, "It's difficult to argue with the old man. Wait for some time; I'll see to it that the box comes to the film archive". A couple of years later, after the death of the old man, the box was deposited at the Archive. Unfortunately, by that time most of the reels had been damaged and we could salvage only a couple of films—*Murliwala* (1927), *Satyavan Savitri* (1927)—produced by the Maharashtra Film Company and directed by Baburao Painter.

The story of how the Archive obtained the films made by the Prabhat Film Company is also interesting. When the government acquired the Company's studio premises in 1960 to set up the Film & Television Institute of India (FTII), they were offered the rights to the Company's films as well. Since it was outside the FTII's mandate to take up the offer, the distributor, Mr Namade of Ulka Film Distributors, was ordered to vacate the studio premises and remove all film prints and negatives at the earliest. Having no other choice, Namade deposited the material at the vaults of the Central Bank of India at Deccan Gymkhana. Unfortunately, in the Panshet Dam disaster of July 1961, the whole vault was filled with water and several films were damaged. A desperate Namade sold whatever he could salvage at a throwaway price to one

The author outside the Jayakar bungalow at the National Film Archive of India, Pune **Image:** NFAI

Mr. Mudaliar from Chennai, who had thought of dubbing Prabhat's classic 'saint films' such as *Sant Tukaram, Sant Dnyaneshwar,* (1940), *Sant Sakhu* (1941) and others into Tamil, Telugu and Kannada for the South Indian market. However, after releasing a couple of titles, he realised that the experiment was not really working.

Meanwhile, the NFAI had commenced its operations and was under pressure from the media to retrieve the Prabhat films, a vital component of India's cinematic heritage. We were compelled to step in and open negotiations with Mudaliar, who proved to be a rather difficult person. Somehow, we managed to strike a deal to copy all the forty-three Prabhat films in Mudaliar's possession, preparing a master positive and a release positive for each film in exchange for a royalty equal to the print cost. To avoid transporting the nitrate negatives, we started on the copying at a couple of laboratories in Chennai. When we had copied around five to six films, Anandrao Damle, the owner of the Prabhat Film Company (and also a son of one of its founder-partners), arrived on the scene. Settling all dues directly, he transferred our contract with Mudaliar to his own name and brought all the film material back to Pune, where it was kept in the Archive's custody. The

work of copying was continued at the FTII's laboratory, which was ironically the former Prabhat lab where the films had once been stored. This is a classic example of the maxim 'penny wise and pound foolish'.

We were more fortunate with the films of another great studio, New Theatres. The studio had lost all its original negatives in a fire in 1939, but the studio boss, B. N. Sircar had promptly called for prints from distributors across the country and ordered dupes. Had it not been for the foresight of this great visionary, films like *Chandidas* (1932), *Devdas* (1936), *Mukti* (1937), *Vidyapati* (1937) and *President* (1937) would not have survived. Sircar later became the first Chairman of the NFAI's Advisory Committee, and he offered all his films free to the Archive.

There were other filmmakers who helped us with advice and information. It was Ritwik Ghatak who arranged for the NFAI to acquire a print of Uday Shankar's *Kalpana* (1948). He informed us that Shankar had a personal print which he could be persuaded to deposit with the Archive. I got in touch with the celebrated dancer and managed to get hold of a dupe negative of his film. It was a great gesture on his part to have deposited it with the Archive at a time when nobody knew much about its operations.

A key initiative taken by the Archive was to acquire films from all over India. I made my first official visit to Chennai, where the Archive was offered nitrate reels of the films *Balayogini* (1937) and *Samsara Nowka* (1936) directed by K. Subramaniam. However, they were in a poor condition and could not be copied. Later the veteran film-maker himself helped us locate the original nitrate reels of his famous film *Thyagabhoomi* (1939) in Mumbai. When I met S. S. Vasan at his Gemini Studios, he offered a print of his film *Chandralekha* (1948) free of cost. He told me that he considered only three of his films—*Chandralekha*, *Avaiyyar* (1953) and *Mr Sampat* (1948)—worth preserving, dismissing the rest of his studio's output as films made purely to earn money. I observed that film-makers had no idea of the historical importance of their popular films, which had entertained large audiences in the country.

Other titles such as *Chintamani* (1937) and *Haridas* (1944) were obtained from Gopalaswamy Ayyengar, one of the biggest distributors of Tamil films. They were copied at his thatched-roof laboratory Tamil Nadu Talkies, the only place that continued to copy nitrate when other labs had switched to safety base. Nemai Ghosh, the Bengali director of *Chinnamul* (1950) who had relocated to Chennai, wanted his famous left-wing film *Pathai Theriayuthu Paar* (1960) preserved in the Archive but the negative could not be located in my time. However, we did manage to acquire other left-wing films made in the South such as *Velaikari* (1949), *Mudhalali* (1958) and *Ratha Kanneer* (1954). Searching for films made by the famous Modern Theatres of Salem, which produced a number of successful Tamil hits in the forties and fifties, we discovered that most of them had been damaged or lost to fire. We did manage to copy the surviving titles such as *Ayiram Thalaivangi Apoorva Chintamoni* (1947) and *Manthri Kumari* (1950) at the studio's Salem lab. I understand that nothing is left of the studio now save the portico at the entrance: a sad commentary on how we treat our heritage.

Starting with a collection of 123 National-Award-winning films in 1964, the Archive's holdings rose to nearly 12,000 titles by the time I retired in 1991. Considering the country's film output, this is still a negligent record, especially as many landmark films remain in the 'permanently lost' list. The search continues... It is possible that films that cannot be found in India may yet turn up in countries like South Africa, Algeria, or countries in the East where Indian films have been shown from the thirties onwards. Three reels of Kanjibhai Rathod's silent film *Sukanya Savitri* (1922) were retrieved from a theatre in Bangkok, through the efforts of Dome Sukwong, head of the Thai archive. We need to identify and collect other such Indian films (and also film material on India) that may be lying abroad. This is an independent research project in itself.

Till recently, prints of old Indian films also used to turn up in Mumbai's Chor Bazaar and other such markets. Often, the new owner's only consideration was what price could be extracted for the prints. Our argument that these were positive prints and that we would need to spend a great deal on the preparation of dupe negatives and on air-conditioned storage usually fell on deaf ears.

Apart from these sources, there are also certain organisations and individuals who have custody of films of historical interest, but lack the technical know-how or wherewithal to preserve them for posterity. For example, the Vishwabharati Foundation, which owns the copyright of all the literary works of the Nobel Laureate Rabindranath Tagore, had a couple of films with which the poet was associated. They approached the Archive and we helped them to restore three reels of the film *Natir Pooja* (The Worship of the Dancing Girl, 1932). The other films, however, were damaged beyond repair. If they had been brought to our notice earlier, perhaps we could have salvaged some of them. There were many such instances of films that could not be saved.

KEY PROBLEMS IN FILM PRESERVATION

Though India can claim to be the world's largest film-making country, the bulk of raw stock used in its cinema is imported. We are dependent on Kodak, Agfa, Orwo, Fuji and other stock coming from abroad. In the sixties, when the NFAI was started, we discovered that many of the negatives of the established film companies from the thirties had lasted, while films made in the forties had suffered the most damage. The reason behind this was that in the war years, much of the material used in manufacturing raw stock was diverted to making parachutes and other items used in war. Such stock as was sent to colonies like India was quite substandard, as we were to discover later. The maximum damage had happened to sound negatives, and later the picture. This was the situation till the beginning of the fifties, when nitrate stock came to be replaced by a more stable and non-inflammable triacetate base.

In the fifties, the normal practice for Hindi film producers was to issue a print order of forty to fifty release prints to the laboratories for all-India distribution. All these prints were taken from the original negatives. Only when the film became a hit and the print order rose to over 300 did the producers care to prepare a dupe negative, on the lab's protest that the original negative would not run any longer on the printing machine. Seldom did producers have the foresight to prepare a dupe negative in the first instance. Their stock reply was that at the time of the release, they had no clue whether the film would be successful or not and how many prints would be required in the final analysis. Therefore, they preferred not to incur any additional expenditure on preparing dupes. This was indeed the 'penny wise, pound foolish' policy again. If their films have survived, it is through sheer luck. The situation has improved since then, and there is consciousness on the part of the producers to take care of their original negatives.

Because the laboratories handled so much work, films that needed repeat washing were not washed properly and there was plenty of left-over 'hypo' (Sodium Sulphate), which damages the film base in due course of time. A white powder appears on the film, which begins to emit a foul smell, while the base stock becomes thin and unsuitable for projection. This is known as the 'vinegar syndrome', which is common with acetate-base films. This syndrome has destroyed many of our films.

FILM RESTORATION AT THE ARCHIVE

During my tenure as the head of the NFAI, I came across films under various stages of deterioration. The film *Chitralekha* (1941) was discovered on a rainy day in a cowshed in Kolkata and brought to Pune. When we opened the cans, we found that the reels were stuck together and hardened like stone. When we started separating the layers of the reels, they broke like mica and crumbled into powder. We had to use all our ingenuity to restore the film. First it was kept in the hot sun for a couple of days and then in an indigenous desiccator. We kept the hardened film reel on a wire mesh and let steam rising from boiling water pass through it so that the reel expanded and its layers began to separate. Next, the reel was put on a winder and turned so that each layer came out slowly till the very last one. Some four or five frames on either side of the central bobbin had become yellow and were damaged. We had to remove these damaged portions and replace them with blank frames. We discovered that the reels were negatives. A film checker was assigned exclusively to the repair work: It took him over one laborious month to complete the salvaging of one reel. With great difficulty we copied the O.K. frames, frame by frame. The work was so strenuous we could copy only one reel, and the other reels had to be put aside for later. (These remaining reels were unfortunately lost in a fire that took place in January 2003).

Very often, damaged films needed to be copied frame by frame in this manner, a method which required an enormous amount of time and patience. Before the advent of digital technology, this is how films were brought back to life. This very method was used to restore *Kaliya Mardan*, one of the few almost complete silent films of Phalke. After the film's material was brought to Pune, the Archive undertook the arduous work of copying it onto safety film. With the help of Phalke's elder son, who had vivid memories of the film, the reels were assembled into a logical order. Eventually, apart from the few damaged portions at the beginning and end of the *Kaliya Mardan* reels we were forced to discard, almost all of the six-reeler was salvaged successfully. The restored print was presented at the Phalke Centenary celebration held in Bombay in 1970, and the Archive's reconstruction work was widely applauded by critics and film historians.

In this instance, the attempt was to restore the film to its original form as far as possible. But what if one is uncertain of the original form? With Indian film-makers, it was a common practice to re-edit the film after the premiere release to make it more acceptable to the mass audience, chopping off portions from the original negatives. There was also an instance in which an artiste filed a suit before the film's public release, forcing the producer to remove her songs from the film. In such cases, it is difficult to say which version is 'original'. Ritwik Ghatak's *Ajantrik* (1958) is another case in point. In 1963-64, when Ghatak visited the FTII for the first time as a guest lecturer, we had a complete retrospective of his work, which included this particular film. Ghatak himself had brought the print, which was a complete version in fourteen reels. In the discussion after the screening, opinions were voiced about a lengthy passage of the film—thirty minutes or so depicting the lifestyle of the Oraon tribals—which had little to do with the main story of the taxi driver and his ramshackle vehicle. Ritwik-da agreed that the length of the film could be reduced. When we copied a fresh print four years later, we discovered that it was only ten reels—a full four reels shorter. Either the producer Pramod Lahiri or Ghatak himself had edited the film, and it is this cutdown version that we have today. I do not know where the removed reels are; they may have been destroyed by now. Perhaps it was the longer version that was shown at the Venice festival, where the film famously caught the attention of the French film critic and historian Georges Sadoul, who declared it a landmark of world cinema.

At times, restorers have deliberately taken it on themselves to go beyond the original film. I can recall one case in which the restoration work involved a conscious effort

Chitralekha (1941): the film that was discovered in a cowshed in Kolkata.

to improve on the original by taking recourse to technology. A well-known producer-director of stunt films in the thirties and forties offered to deposit his old material with the Archive, asking for some raw stock to correct the negatives. Later we came to know that he had re-edited the film, transferred the sound optically to improve its quality and inserted titles to explain the historical importance of the film. When we asked the producer about his 'improvements', he replied he wanted to make the film presentable and acceptable to modern audiences. As the copyright owner, he was of course within his rights to do so, but I believe that he should have altered the film only after allowing the Archive to make a dupe negative or positive copy of the original.

Tampering with the original work poses several moral and ethical issues. For instance, Satyajit Ray's *Pather Panchali* (1955) was shot with various cameras and recording equipment over a three-year period. Though the film was technically uneven in picture and sound quality, it went on to be recognised as a great world classic. Its technical deficiencies today stand as an eloquent testimony to the filmmaker's struggle to create his work. Surely, a flawless digital restoration which removed these deficiencies entirely would be erasing a part of the film's history as well.

I believe that the ethics of film preservation and restoration make it incumbent on the archivist to take care of the material deposited with the archive in such a way that any future presentation is as true to the original as possible. Any conscious attempt to tamper with the original is quite dangerous and ethically incorrect. The film archive involved in restoration work should strike a balance between its basic responsibility of preservation for the historical record and the cultural objective of presentation to a contemporary audience. Both the objectives should complement each other and not work at cross-purposes. This is indeed the great challenge before all film archivists.

Founder and former Director of the National Film Archive of India (NFAI), P.K. Nair is a film archivist of long standing who pioneered film preservation in India. He was associated with the NFAI for nearly three decades, building it up from scratch to an institution of international reckoning.

Chitralekha (1964), Eastmancolor. An example of colour fading to red as a result of deterioration in a colour print **Courtesy**: Vikram Sharma

THE MAGIC OF CELLULOID

SHIVENDRA SINGH DUNGARPUR

Walking through a maze of alleys in Pathanwadi, a slum in the suburbs of Mumbai, I am being taken by my guide Bipin 'Silver' to the place where films go to die. Bipin Silver has earned his name from his choice of livelihood, extracting silver from black-and-white films. He has brought me here on one condition: he will not come in front of the camera.

I duck down through the narrow door of a tin shed into a dark room in which there are two drums, an old film winder and strips of film hanging from makeshift bamboo poles. A door leads into another room piled high with 16 mm and 35 mm film cans, all awaiting their funeral. I watch in fascinated horror as a thin old man systematically strips these films bare of silver, of cinema, of memories, leaving ghostly translucent white strips of nothing scattered on the floor.

So what is a film worth in terms of silver? Bipin says he strips 1000 kgs of film in one go, 50 films stripped bare to extract 3 kgs of silver. As a silver scavenger, his personal preference is nitrate, which is a better source for silver than safety film. And he has been doing this for the last forty years!

Growing up, I always thought film would last forever. Somehow I has never thought that these images, which seemed so much larger than life on the screen and evoked such powerful emotions, actually had such a fragile existence. That they can disappear in a matter of minutes is disturbing; it is as if someone were to take away my own memories.

I think I must have first fallen in love with celluloid when I was a child spending my summer vacations with my maternal grandparents at their home in Dumraon, Bihar. Every evening, the family would gather on the verandah to watch a film. I have vivid memories of the projectionist Chandi Mistry cycling up to the house as the sun went down and setting up the projector as I waited impatiently for the show to begin. I would be asked to choose the films for the evening's show, and I would run into the living room, which everyone called the *thanda* room, because it was the one air-conditioned room in the house. There, I would stand before the glass-fronted cabinet which was full of film cans—16 mm films of my parents' wedding and my grandparents' travels in India and abroad; 8 mm films of Chaplin, Laurel & Hardy, and Buster Keaton... I can still smell the film, just as I did all those years ago when I opened the cabinet. I would hold up the strips of film to the light and examine the tiny images that sprang to life on the screen when the film threaded its way through the projector. It was magic. Even the burning of the films as they got stuck in the gate of the projector fascinated me. That Bolex Paillard projector, gifted to me by my grandfather, is one of my prized possessions even today.

But the real highlight of the holidays was watching films with my grandmother at the local cinema hall. This was an unforgettable experience. We would travel in a blue Matador van to the cinema, where my grandmother would have booked the entire theatre for us to watch films back-to-back the whole day. We would sit in the stalls, tiny figures in the darkened hall, silhouetted against the flickering images on the big screen. I would keep looking over my shoulder at the rays of light coming from the projection room, which mysteriously transformed into the story unfolding in front of us on the screen. In the interval, I would be taken up to the projection room where I would watch spellbound as the projectionist wound and rewound

Films being stripped for silver at Pathanwadi, Goregaon, Mumbai. From *Celluloid Man* (2012)

the films, and at times even spliced together some of the joints. Sometimes a man would rush in to grab a few cans and race off with them to another cinema on his bicycle.

People are talking these days about the death of celluloid. For me this is a very emotional topic, since I think of celluloid as a living, breathing medium, with its own unique depth, sound and feel. Having explored its textures as a filmmaker, I was struck by how ephemeral the life of one's creations could be if they were not preserved. I was drawn towards exploring this aspect of celluloid, and my documentary *Celluloid Man* (2012) was the result. The making of my film was a journey of discovery of the vanishing legacy of Indian cinema and its butterfly existence.

The journey of Indian cinema began with the release of Dadasaheb Phalke's *Raja Harishchandra* on May 3, 1913. Phalke advertised the four-reel film with this copy: "A performance with 57000 photographs. A picture 2 miles long. All for three annas." Today, of Phalke's wonderful two-mile long film, only one mile remains.

The destruction of our celluloid legacy proceeds from here into more horrifying statistics: of the 1700 silent films made in India, the National Film Archive of India (NFAI) has only five or six films, none really complete, and another ten or twelve in fragments, some as short as

149 feet. Of the 124 films and 38 documentaries produced by the film industry in Chennai (formerly Madras), only one film survives, the 1931 film *Marthanda Verma*. By 1950, we had lost 70 to 80 per cent of our films. This is excluding the numerous missing short films, animation films, television programmes, advertising commercials, home movies, etc., often forgotten in the shadow of the silver screen, which form an important part of the fabric of our visual history.

It was half a century after cinema began in India, when the devastating loss of its history and the need for an archive was recognised. By the time the NFAI was set up in 1964 under its pioneering director P. K. Nair, there were already gaping holes in the record. A few more figures may help put the loss into perspective. According to the latest figures released by the Central Board of Film Certification, in 2013 alone, India produced 1724 films in 32 languages, of which 744 films were shot on celluloid. This is the output of a single year in Indian film history. Set this against the fact that after 100 years of cinema in India, and 50 years of operation for the NFAI, the archive has just about 6000 Indian film titles in their collection, and it becomes quite evident that very little of our film legacy has been preserved.

How and when did we lose so many of our films? For early films, one significant reason is the highly inflammable nature of the material on which they were shot. Before

1951, most films were shot on cellulose nitrate base, using the same material from which gunpowder is made. This nitrate base was first introduced by George Eastman of Kodak as it gave black-and-white images of a higher quality than the glass negatives used at the time. Edison began using it to record motion pictures as well. However, as nitrate stock came to be widely adopted, people began to realise that it was highly undependable. If stored in damp conditions, nitrate could decompose and if stored in the heat, it could ignite on its own.

Many early nitrate films were destroyed in fires in vaults, studios and even during projection, till the advent of a more stable base, cellulose acetate, which is known as safety film. India's first feature film, Phalke's *Raja Harishchandra* was lost to fire, forcing Phalke to reshoot the film in 1917; another fire that year in a Kolkata warehouse destroyed around forty films made by the pioneer Hiralal Sen. During the Second World War, a major fire took place at B.N. Sircar's New Theatres in Kolkata, resulting in the loss of many of the original camera negatives of their celebrated productions, among them *Chandidas* (1932) and *Devdas* (1935). As recently as January 8, 2003, there was a fire at the Film and Television Institute of India (FTII) in Pune. Here, in premises that were once the studios of the great Prabhat Film Company, nitrate flames devoured 45 original negatives of Prabhat classics such as *Amar Jyoti* (1936), *Amrit Manthan* (1934) and *Sant Tukaram* (1936), besides prints of rare silent films such as *Raja Harishchandra* and *Kaliya Mardan* (1919) that had been collected from the Phalke family.

The fire story that set the rumour mills buzzing in the late 1940s was when the Ranjit Movietone warehouse in Mumbai went up in flames. The word on the street was that it was a clever insurance scam perpetrated by the studio head, Chandulal Shah, who had lost heavily at the races and was up to his neck in debt. Indian cinema lost almost 150 films of the thirties and forties in the fire, many of them popular box-office hits. Among the films lost were matinee star K.L. Saigal's *Bhakt Surdas* (1942) and the well-known classic *Holi* (1940) directed by A.R. Kardar. A mere handful of productions from the Ranjit banner survive today.

The fifties saw another major nitrate fire in Mumbai. At the time, Famous Cine Lab, Tardeo, had 40 to 50 warehouses in various parts of the city where they stored their films; in the outlying suburb of Malad alone they had 24 godowns where nitrate films were stored. It was their godown at the Rajabahadur Motilal Mills in Tardeo which was struck by fire, gutting several nitrate films.

Actor and director Dev Anand, who was editing his film *Funtoosh* (1956) next door at the Famous Cine Lab, had an unusual reaction to the event. Since his film required shots of a fire, he seized the opportunity to rush over and take shots of the inferno. If you watch the film today, you can see for yourself how the nitrate films burned that day at the Famous Cine Lab warehouse.

Another fire of the early fifties was at the vaults of the South India Film Chamber of Commerce, which held negatives of the films of various South producers. Original nitrate negatives of 70 to 80 films were lost in a matter of hours. Such occurrences were frequent enough that the Department of Explosives headquartered at Nagpur made it mandatory for labs and producers to obtain special permission to store nitrate films. The department also issued directives on how to store films, which were to be followed strictly in order to get a licence.

After 1951, when producers began to adopt cellulose acetate (considered more stable and non-inflammable than nitrate both in terms of usage and storage) many nitrate prints were transferred to the new 'safety film'. However, cellulose acetate had its own problems, being prone to a form of decay known as 'vinegar syndrome'. If cellulose acetate is not stored in humidity-controlled conditions at the correct temperature, it tends to deteriorate: a process characterised by shrinkage, brittleness and buckling of the emulsion, as well a pungent smell of vinegar. To counter this problem, polyester base was developed for all print films, duplicating films and some specialty films. Since the storage life of polyester base is ten times that of safety base, it became popular for striking prints (cellulose acetate is still used to shoot films, since polyester base can damage camera equipment).

Meanwhile, colour films brought in a fresh set of problems: if prints were not stored properly, after a while the colours would fade to red. This was unfortunate, since for many Indian producers, storage meant dumping cans in warehouses without any facilities for temperature control. India's film industries developed in the three major colonial port cities of Bombay, Madras and Calcutta (now Mumbai, Chennai and Kolkata), where climactic conditions were not ideal for preserving films. Thus, high humidity and temperature levels took their inevitable toll. Those producers who stored their films in laboratories faced another kind of problem. The usual practice was for producers to pay an annual deposit fee to a laboratory to store the original camera negative of the film. However, if the film had not been a great success, the producers would sooner or later stop paying the deposit

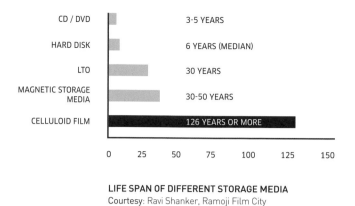

LIFE SPAN OF DIFFERENT STORAGE MEDIA
Courtesy: Ravi Shanker, Ramoji Film City

fee, resulting in the labs dispatching the cans to some old warehouse, where storage conditions would be less than ideal.

The advent of television in India in the 1970s saw producers scrambling to look for these very film cans, when they realised that there was still money to be made out of old films. For many films, it was too late by then. This era also saw the introduction of U-matic tape, and later, Betacam. Producers enthusiastically transferred their films onto the new formats and discarded their original negatives, drawn to what they thought was a cheaper and more convenient option for storage. What they did not realise was that far from being an ideal mode of preservation, video lacked the longevity of celluloid, and was also poorer in image quality. However, the damage was done: in the absence of original camera negatives, it is these inferior copies from the eighties that are being used till date as source material by Indian DVD and VCD companies for their releases. The legacy of poor picture and sound quality is now spreading like a virus on the internet. Unfortunately, as we enter the digital age, we seem to have failed to learn from our earlier mistakes. Even today, we are enthusiastically discarding celluloid for low-resolution digital, ignoring the fact that celluloid is the only proven archival medium with a lifespan of a century, while the longevity of digital formats remains unproven and untested.

———————

Standing under the widespread branches of an old tree in Mumbai's Jyoti Studio, P.K. Nair told me the tragic story of *Alam Ara* (1931) India's first sound film, which had been shot by Ardeshir Irani in that very place. Mr. Nair visited the director in 1970 to persuade him to archive his landmark film. Irani pointed to a few cans lying in his office and told Mr. Nair he was free to take them to the Archive. But when Irani's son Shapur was escorting him down the stairs, he confessed that he had sold the film

for silver a long time ago without his father's knowledge, and only the cans remained. As a true archivist, Mr. Nair still lives in the hope that this film will be found somewhere in some part of the world, like the John Ford film *Upstream* discovered in New Zealand, or the lost Chaplin film *Thief Catcher* that was found in an antique fair in Michigan.

The *Alam Ara* story illustrates another reason behind the obliteration of our film heritage. Photochemical processes and changes in technology alone are not to blame: a combination of greed, apathy and negligence is equally responsible. Silver scavenging itself may go back to the early years of Indian cinema: journalist and editor Baburao Patel refers to the practice in a 1935 *Filmindia* piece about the film *Chandidas*. "When all the films are melted down to yield silver, let us preserve *Chandidas* for posterity," he writes, "Not because it made history, but because it failed to do so". A generation before the founding of the NFAI, here is an awareness of the need to preserve even neglected films, a prescient plea for art to prevail over commerce.

As for apathy, there are numerous examples from over the years. When the Bombay Film Laboratories Pvt. Ltd., one

Zubeida (star of the first Indian talkie *Alam Ara*) in the silent film *Veer Abhimanyu* (1922) **Courtesy:** Nikhil Dhanrajgir

of the biggest processing labs in Mumbai, was shutting down in 2004, they put out large public notices in various trade publications, asking producers to collect their negatives, or else the "the same will be disposed off as hazardous waste at the disposal facilities at Taloja of the Mumbai Waste Management Ltd." Though the notices appeared 13 times in all, few producers—7-8% of them at best—came forward to collect their films. Thanks to the producers' disregard, many cinematic gems were literally consigned to the rubbish heap.

There are several instances, too, of producers abandoning their films like so many unwanted babies. On a visit to the NFAI, I noticed a huge pile of film cans lying in the basement near the vaults. I was curious to know where they had come from. When I asked the Film Preservation Officer, he told me an interesting story about how Indian Railways has been an unwitting contributor to the film archive movement in India. After a film had had its run at the box office, producers often found themselves with several prints in hand. Not knowing what to do with them, they would consign them via the Railways with no clear destination marked. By law, it fell on the Railways to dispose of unclaimed prints, and that was how thousands of orphaned cans ultimately found their way to the NFAI.

While nitrate fires, silver extraction, vinegar syndrome and the like have been responsible for much damage, and attitudes of apathy and neglect are equally to blame, to my mind the root cause of India's tragic loss of its cinematic heritage is the way cinema has always been regarded in this country. It has been viewed merely as a medium of mass entertainment, and never as an art form integral to our social and cultural fabric.

I believe that while film may be a relatively new art form, it is deeply rooted in our culture. In India, we can go back 30,000 years in time to the cave paintings of Bhimbetka in Central India. I remember my father taking me to the caves when I was a schoolboy. You entered the darkness of the cave, and when you saw the paintings, they gave you a feeling of motion and time, and a sense of who these people were and where they came from. The paintings showed daily life, but they drew you far beyond the depiction to imagine what was not shown. That is the power of imagination, which goes beyond reality to create an illusion, and that is what cinema is.

India also has a long tradition of pictorial story-telling, seen in folk art forms such as Chitrakathi (lit. 'picture story'). Here, narrative images were painted in a series on a long scroll, which would be held up as a performer

PUBLIC NOTICE

Re: **Negatives of very old Black & White Films with BOMBAY FILM LABORATORIES PVT. LTD.**

Negatives of about 200 very old films produced **MORE THAN 40 YEARS** ago are lying at the Chembur Godowns of **BOMBAY FILM LABORATORIES PVT. LTD.** in a highly decomposed and unidentifiable condition. A list of these films is available for inspection at the Administrative Office of Bombay Film Laboratories Pvt. Ltd. at 149, S.K. Bole Road, Dadar, Mumbai 400 028 by prior appointment on telephone no. 24222510.

Any person who has any right, title or interest in any of these films is hereby given **NOTICE** that he is required to collect the negative he owns after complying with all legal requirements and after making payment of the amount due to the Company including storage charges **WITHIN ONE MONTH** from the publication of this Notice **FAILING WHICH** the negatives **WILL BE DISPOSED OFF AS JUNK** and thereafter no claim of any nature will be entertained by the Company.

Dated this 28th day of January 2004.

BOMBAY FILM LABORATORIES PVT. LTD.
(Now known as **RAHEJA PRINCESS APARTMENTS PVT. LTD.**)

Public Notice issued by Bombay Laboratories Pvt. Ltd. in *Film Information*, January 31, 2004 **Courtesy**: Hosi Wadia

(sometimes the artist himself) recited the story with the aid of this visual support. Again, this is not far removed from cinema. When film was introduced to India, its artists were quick to recognise its kinship with Indian tradition, as well as its uniqueness as a mode of expression. The poet Rabindranath Tagore observed, "The principal element of a motion picture is the flux of images. The beauty and grandeur of this form in motion has to be developed in such a way that it becomes self-sufficient without the use of words".

Notir Puja (1932) was Tagore's own experiment with film (he had earlier written the intertitles for Modhu Bose's 1930 film *Giribala*). In the 1930s, other great literary figures such as Saadat Hassan Manto and Munshi Premchand were drawn to the film industry in Bombay, writing scripts for films like *Kisan Kanya* (1936) and *Mazdoor* (a.k.a. *The Mill*, 1934) respectively. Artists such as M.F. Husain (who made his first film *Through the Eyes of a Painter* in 1967) and legendary musicians such as Pandit Ravi Shankar, Ustad Vilayat Khan, Bade Ghulam Ali Khan, Ali Akbar Khan and renowned Carnatic vocalist M.S. Subbulakshmi have all collaborated on films.

And yet, India does not recognise cinema, which is so

My Chor Bazaar friend Shahid with the only existing song booklet of *Alam Ara* (1931)

much a part of our culture, as an art. Mahatma Gandhi included it among evils like gambling and horse-racing which he wanted to banish: an essentially hostile attitude which was shared by the orthodox and conservative elements of Indian society. Even today, India's Constitution mentions cinema under entry 62 in the Seventh Schedule of the State List, which deals with "taxes on luxuries, including taxes on entertainments, amusements, betting and gambling." Current Indian legislation dealing with cinema focusses primarily on censorship and taxation, and these subjects dictate the dialogue of the film industry with the government.

Given these attitudes, it is obvious that film preservation has never been a priority for the government. At a time when no one seemed to care about the future of Indian cinema's past, we were fortunate to have a true cinephile like P. K. Nair at the helm of the NFAI. He literally built the archive can by can during his 27-year career. I first got to know him when I was a student at the FTII in Pune. He was the only person I knew who could tell you exactly in which reel a particular scene from a film could be found. It was almost like a game to ask him a question; he was always right.

Had it not been for Mr. Nair, early pioneers like Phalke, Damle and Fatehlal, Debaki Bose, P.C. Barua and Shantaram would have been mere names that appeared in history books. India has also had unsung archivists like Abdul Ali, a film-lover who singlehandedly assisted the NFAI in retrieving over 350 films. Amongst the films he salvaged from warehouses across the country were milestone films like *Achhut Kanya* (1936) and *Izzat* (1937) directed by Franz Osten for the Bombay Talkies banner. He recovered the iconic film *Mahal* (1949), directed by Kamal Amrohi, from the Official Liquidator's office and re-released it at the Roxy Cinema in Mumbai in the seventies, when it had a second successful run for ten weeks.

One of my favourite haunts in Mumbai is the infamous Chor Bazaar or 'Thieves' Market'. One of the largest flea markets in India, it is a treasure trove of the country's film history. I often walk the narrow lanes, stopping for a cup of tea and a chat with my friends Shahid, Aziz, Arif and Iqbal who have had shops here for generations, selling rare film memorabilia and other artefacts. Films are sold here by the kilo: 8 mm films for Rs. 300 per reel; entire films on 16 mm for Rs. 4000; and 35 mm films for Rs. 100 per kg. Once I even managed to acquire an original camera negative of the film *Bharosa* (1963) starring Guru Dutt that had been discarded by a lab. Through a strange paradox, Chor Bazaar has unwittingly become an archive of Indian cinema, where even today one can find rare prizes like the only known song booklet of the film *Alam Ara*. Sadly, the end is nigh for Chor Bazaar: the neighbourhood is slated for redevelopment and one day, nothing will remain of these old streets.

———————

In some respects, film preservation in India owes more to the Chor Bazaars and the passionate collectors who trawl their streets, than it does to the film industry itself. The country has nearly ten different film industries producing the largest number of films in the world, with the four major South Indian film industries accounting for nearly 60% of the total film production. The mega stars of these industries went on to head governments in these states, but did very little for the cause of preserving their cinematic history. Today the NFAI remains India's only film archive. In the absence of a mandatory deposit system, the NFAI, with its limited funding and inadequately trained staff, is hard pressed to cope.

Today the industry is turning its back on celluloid in a definite drift towards digital technology, reinforcing the belief that the original camera negative is an obsolete artefact from another era. This arises from widespread ignorance amongst filmmakers, copyright-holders and industry stake-holders. Labs are shutting down all over the country (including Kodak, which shut down at the end of 2014) and discarding film cans on the scrap heap, as producers are not interested in taking possession of their films. None of the Indian entities engaged in film restoration today have photochemical facilities. Producers, copyright-holders and the public at large are quite satisfied with basic digital restoration, done at a low cost. There is a general lack of understanding that a full-fledged film restoration goes beyond just digital scanning and cleaning, and must include the repair and restoration of the original source material.

It is high time we realise that we need to take urgent steps to preserve every bit of our cinematic history before it is too late. A film like *Kaagaz ke Phool*, for instance, was not successful at the box office when it was first released, but was acclaimed in the 1980s, when it was revived at

film societies. Similarly, the Fearless Nadia films made by Wadia Movietone were seen as B-grade stunt films earlier, but today are considered classics. Every kind of film has to be preserved, so that future generations have the opportunity to assess them and find new values in them. We should aim to preserve not just feature films, but all forms of the moving image including documentaries, newsreels, experimental and avant-garde films, television content, advertising films, music videos, etc.

A national plan must be implemented to save Indian films and make them more accessible to the public. Greater public-private partnership should be the focus of the plan as it is only with the efforts of the film community and the support of the public that significant progress can be made to save our cinematic heritage. The government should recognise the moving image as an art form and a record of our times. It should take the lead by allotting funds for film preservation and restoration and also offering incentives to the film industry that will encourage them to take up the cause of saving our film heritage.

The National Film Archive of India should be made an autonomous body and run by qualified and trained archivists who understand the importance of celluloid, and are aware of the constantly evolving digital technology. Each film industry in the country should have its own regional archive, which should have a mandatory acquisition policy. Film storage facilities need to be improved, expanded and optimised, as saving the original source material of films is of utmost importance.

Preservation is just the first step. Films are meant for the public at large, and archives should go beyond just warehousing. A detailed inventory and classification of the films in the archives must be done to facilitate public access for purposes of reference and research. While these are practical measures to put the preservation of film heritage on the cultural map, the real challenge will be to change the age-old attitude which regards cinema as mere entertainment.

India has a singular cinematic legacy that is endangered. What is lost, we need to find; what we have, we need to restore; and what we create, we need to preserve for tomorrow. It's time we recognised cinema as a national treasure, one that must be saved and protected.

Shivendra Singh Dungarpur is a filmmaker, archivist, and the director of the documentary Celluloid Man *(2012). He is the Founder-Director of the Film Heritage Foundation, which works towards preserving India's cinematic heritage.*

RESTORING INDIAN TREASURES:
THREE CASE STUDIES

A still from *Kalpana* (1948) **Courtesy:** Amala Shankar

UDAY SHANKAR'S *KALPANA*
CECILIA CENCIARELLI

When I am on the stage I seem to be in a temple. What I do is an act of worship.
Uday Shankar

"If he performs in Geneva, don't miss going there," wrote James Joyce to his daughter Lucia from Paris in June 1934, referring to Uday Shankar. "He moves on the stage floor like some divine being... believe me, there are still some beautiful things in this poor old world." Lucia Joyce was a ballet dancer training with experimental dancer Isadora Duncan, around the time Uday Shankar was achieving his fame in Europe. In the early twenties, the famous Russian prima ballerina Anna Pavlova had just returned to London from a tour of East Asia and India when she was introduced to Uday, who had recently moved to England with his family. Inspired by her trip, Pavlova was working on three miniature ballets: *Ajanta Frescoes*, *A Hindu Wedding* and *Krishna and Radha*. Apparently, Pavlova was immediately captured by Uday's talent and asked him to choreograph the first two ballets for her, and to partner her in *Krishna and Radha*. Shankar's choreography drew from his experiences of life in Rajasthan. The following year, Pavlova's performances of these pieces at the Royal Opera House in Covent Garden received enthusiastic notices and soon after, Pavlova asked Shankar to join her on her American tour in 1923. Within ten years, Uday Shankar took his own ballet to the United States, and by the mid-forties he was acknowledged as a major figure in the history of Indian dance. His style was considered as unique at the time as it is nowadays: classical in spirit, but innovative and free. His synthesis of western theatrical techniques and Indian dance made his art hugely popular both in India and the West.

At the end of the thirties, Uday established his own dance academy in the Himalayas and assembled an impressive group of gifted artists—musicians, dancers, gurus— to join him, among them Guru Dutt, Shanti Bardhan, Simkie (Simone Barbier), Zohra Sehgal, Shanta Gandhi and his own brothers Rajendra, Debendra and Ravi. Before becoming a sitar virtuoso responsible for popularising Hindustani classical music in the West, 13-year-old Ravi Shankar had already joined Uday's dance group, accompanied its members on tour, and learned to dance and play various Indian instruments.

It is actually thanks to Ravi Shankar and to Martin Scorsese's cinephilic appetite and restless engagement in film preservation that *Kalpana* (1948), the only film Uday ever made, and the only record of his hypnotic dance, has been saved for posterity and is now enjoying a new life on the big screen. Ravi Shankar discussed *Kalpana* with Martin Scorsese at the beginning of 2008, when the filmmaker was preparing a new documentary on George Harrison's life and art. Harrison had been a student of Ravi in the late sixties, and their friendship and artistic collaboration continued throughout their lives. "A great work of hallucinatory, homemade expressionism and ecstatic beauty," wrote Scorsese after he watched *Kalpana*. "One of the few real 'dance films', a film that doesn't just include dance sequences, but whose primary physical vocabulary is dance [...] a creative peak in the history of independent Indian filmmaking."

Shankar recruited most of his cast in Kerala; practically all the artists were new, including a 17-year-old Padmini in her debut film. According to the records available, Shankar took roughly 90 days to shoot all the dance sequences, of which there were over 80. All the songs in the film were sung live and accompanied by an orchestra playing Indian instruments. At the time of its release in 1948, the film received enthusiastic acclaim in India and abroad: "Shankar has not only vindicated his reputation as a great showman and a great dancer, but through this picture also thrown a challenge to the film industry," reads a piece on *Kalpana* which appeared in *Filmindia* in March 1948 in response to Shankar's detractors, who had predicted that the film was going to be an "amateurish flop". "Leave aside dancing, which is his own domain, let them come forward and produce something better in technique, in production value, in slick direction, in imaginative photography, in artistic compositions, in daring montage! *Kalpana* is a landmark in the history of Indian films in the same way *Citizen Kane* was in Hollywood. It breaks completely with all the traditions of the Indian cinema, discards all existing formulae, breaks new and virgin ground. It presents a new theme in a novel manner. It presents new artists, new musicians, new writers and new technicians. What is more, its whole approach to the art of cinema is new and different from anything you have ever seen on the screen—Indian or foreign!" Despite garnering similar critical praise in America and Europe alike, receiving a number of awards and being shown by film archives, the film was a commercial failure.

Today, the significance of *Kalpana* appears manifold and despite its cultural specificity, the film speaks to audiences in a universal way. It is remarkable not only for Shankar's artistic vision and choreographing genius, but for the way he depicts society and its contradictions as well as the artist's never-ending conflict with his surroundings. Shankar made his intentions and ambitions very clear in the preamble of the film: "I request you all to be very alert while you watch this unusual picture—a Fantasy. Some of the events depicted here will reel off at great speed and if you miss any piece you will really be missing a vital aspect of our country's life in its Religion, Politics, Education, Society, Art and Culture, Agriculture and Industry. I do not deliberately aim my criticism at any particular group of people or institutions, but if it appears so, it just happens to be so, that is all. It is my duty as an artist to be fully alive to all conditions of life and thought relating to our country and present it truthfully with all the faults and merits through the medium of my Art. And I hope that you will be with me in our final purpose to rectify our own shortcomings and become worthy of our cultural heritage and make our motherland once again the greatest in the world."

In 2008, the World Cinema Project (a special programme within The Film Foundation) created by Martin Scorsese to support the restoration, preservation and dissemination of neglected film patrimony around the world, started considering a possible restoration of *Kalpana*. The uniqueness of the film, virtually unknown in the Western world, unavailable for distribution and rarely screened in its home country, made it a valid candidate for investigating its state of preservation. In partnership with Cineteca di Bologna, the World Cinema Project began a long and complex research process that took over a year.

In a time when technological possibilities are virtually unlimited, it is getting increasingly difficult to dissipate the misconception that restoration is simply about applying the latest technological tools available to make an 'old film' look like new. The task of restoration involves studying the film and its production history, understanding the filmmaker's vision or his limitations, knowing the work of the cinematographer, the designer, the costume maker etc., all of which contributes to making the right choices and adhering to the intentions of the film's creator. Gathering all existing film and non-film sources is the next crucial step of the restoration process, which allows one to compare the available material and establish the most appropriate work-flow. To try and locate material pertaining to *Kalpana* outside of India, a worldwide quest was launched through the International Federation of Film Archives (FIAF) in which over a hundred leading international archives were approached. At the same time, we got in touch with the National Film Archive of India (NFAI) in Pune, which we assumed had most likely preserved at least a circulating print of *Kalpana*. Later on, when we were able to access the voluminous official correspondence filed on the film, we discovered that Uday Shankar had written to the NFAI in 1967, announcing that he was going to donate a dupe negative copy of *Kalpana* for loan and preservation purposes. Since that year, and continuing after Shankar's death in 1977, the NFAI had preserved the dupe negative, which was also periodically used to make new circulating prints.

While *Kalpana* was shot entirely at the Gemini Studios in Chennai (formerly Madras), there were no records to suggest where the film was developed at the time. The fact that Uday Shankar made no reference to an original negative in his letter leads us to believe that it might have been already destroyed or lost by 1967. Nevertheless, we decided to search all the major and oldest laboratories in

Kolkata and Mumbai, unfortunately with no result.

The 35 mm circulating print of *Kalpana* that we viewed at the NFAI in the fall of 2008 showed visible signs of dust and wear, in all probability due to previous screenings, as well as numerous vertical scratches, which were also evident in the dupe negative we inspected. The inspection could not be completed due to the lack of tools like a diascope, preventing us from assessing whether other problems affecting the 35 mm print, such as focus issues, could be attributed to a defective printing process or were present in the dupe negative. Also—a rather frequent occurrence with combined dupe negatives—the optical sound of the positive print was quite damaged.

The rather poor state of the available material and the lack of the original negative was not the only obstacle to the restoration: establishing the rights-owner of *Kalpana* seemed an insurmountable task. The late Vijay Jadav, then the director of the NFAI, informed us that in 1998 a lawsuit had been filed at the High Court of Kolkata involving four different individuals (all women) claiming copyright over the film. So despite the fact that *Kalpana* was, according to Indian law, in the public domain, neither the restoration, nor a simple screening of the film could be authorised. The NFAI and the World Cinema Project jointly submitted the matter to the Minister of Information and Broadcasting in New Delhi who could have a final say in this impasse, but despite the support of filmmakers like Deepa Mehta who fully and generously embraced our call and wrote one letter after another to Indian high officials, nothing happened for several months.

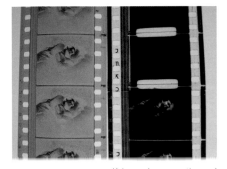

And then, late in 2009, we were approached by Ravi Shankar's wife Sukanya who informed us that the legal dispute was solved and that Amala and Mamata Shankar, Uday's wife and daughter respectively, had been recognised as the sole rights-owners of *Kalpana*. Amala, then 93 years old, had been Uday's long-time dancing partner, and her daughter Mamata too is a dancer and actress. We were thrilled to learn that this endangered film finally belonged to those who were keeping Uday Shankar's artistic legacy alive. Nonetheless, by mid-2010, more legal hurdles stalled the project again. It was only thanks to the generosity, commitment and persistence of Shivendra Singh Dungarpur that *Kalpana* could finally be restored. In 2011, Shivendra brought on board P. K. Nair, founder and director of the National Film Archive of India in 1964, who had been instrumental in acquiring for the archive, over three decades, landmark Indian films such as Dadasaheb Phalke's *Raja Harishchandra* and *Kaliya Mardan*, Bombay Talkies films such as *Jeevan Naiya, Bandhan,* and *Achhut Kanya,* and S. S. Vasan's *Chandralekha.* It was to P. K. Nair that Uday Shankar had entrusted the only existing dupe negative of *Kalpana* in 1967.

In January 2012 the combined dupe negative of *Kalpana* was finally shipped to Cineteca di Bologna in Italy. The staff of L'Immagine Ritrovata laboratory inspected the material: the third-generation dupe negative consisted of 16 reels printed on Orwo film stock. The dupe negative was contact-printed, as confirmed by signs of the original Kodak nitrate negative film stock on the dupe negative itself. Following the inspection, the lab technician proceeded with the physical repair. The dupe negative presented a shrinkage of approximately 0.6%. Some of the splices were dirty or presented signs of decay. A careful manual check and cleaning was performed and re-splicing was carried out

Kalpana, positive print, missing frames

Kalpana, dupe negative before and after repair of critical tear

Kalpana, dupe negative and positive print compared

Images: L'Immagine Ritrovata

using unperforated clear tape and manually opening the perforation with a scalpel. (The use of unperforated tape guarantees extreme precision and ensures that the frame area is invaded as little as possible).

The dupe negative was subsequently scanned at 2K with Arriscan - Archive GUI, a machine specifically designed for archive film scans which allows the disabling of the pin registration for shrunken film material, and enables one to adjust the framing even while the scan is happening, to vary the winding speed and so on. The files produced during this step were, as usual, acquired with no correction, in other words 'raw': this is a very crucial factor to guarantee the full reversibility of the restoration, one of the key concepts within the ethics of restoration[1].

Over 4,000 hours of manual digital restoration were performed, removing more than half a decade's worth of dirt, scratches and splice marks; correcting flickering, jittering and tilting; and fixing a generally unstable image. Grading was carried out using a vintage print as a reference and aimed at recovering the natural sharpness and brightness of the blacks and whites. As usual, the digital files were backed up at every stage of the restoration, both before and after the digital restoration and the grading were performed. Work on sound restoration was also extensive, the dupe negative suffering from duplication causing noise, scratches and crackles. The original sound was digitally transferred from the combined dupe negative and digital cleaning and background noise reduction was applied. The restoration generated a dupe negative, a new optical soundtrack negative for preservation as well as a complete back-up of all the files produced by the digital restoration. A new 35 mm internegative was produced for long-time preservation as well as a complete set of formats for circulation.

Over four years after the project was first launched, the restoration of *Kalpana* premiered at Cannes Classics on May 17, 2012, in the presence of Uday Shankar's widow Amala who also starred as the female lead in the film. The film has since then been screened in festivals around the world. Thanks to this restoration, it has entered its second life on the big screen, revealing Uday Shankar's mesmerising dance and a forgotten treasure of Indian cinema to the world.

RITWIK GHATAK'S *TITAS EKTI NADIR NAAM*
CECILIA CENCIARELLI

The primary objective of making films is to do good to mankind. If you do not do good to humanity, no art is a true work of art. Rabindranath said that art must be faithful to truth first and to beauty secondarily. This truth comes out of an artist's own perceptions and meditations. [...] Art is not a trivial thing. Ritwik Ghatak

In 2009, when we thought that our project of restoring *Kalpana* had reached a stalemate, we were reminded that restoration is often a very human affair, determined by casual encounters and chance. A combination of events led to our getting in touch with film director Ritwik Ghatak's son Ritaban in Kolkata. Restoring Ghatak's works had always been an aspiration. The uniqueness of his voice, the avant-garde quality of some of his works and the intensity of the cinematic experiences produced by his vision make it hard to believe how little Ghatak's films are known. According to filmmaker Deepa Mehta, a die-hard fan of Ghatak, it was perhaps because of the political clamour surrounding much of his work, that the work itself (as opposed to the man's personality and politics) got neglected in India and abroad. As Jacob Levich put it, "If Satyajit Ray was the suitable boy of Indian art cinema—unthreatening, career-oriented, reliably tasteful—Ritwik Ghatak was its problem child. Where Ray's films are seamless, exquisitely rendered conventional narratives that aim for the kind of psychological insights prized by 19th century novelists, Ghatak's are ragged, provisional, intensely personal, yet epic in scale, scope and aspirations [...] viewing Ghatak is an edgy, intimate experience, an engagement with a brilliantly erratic intelligence in an atmosphere of inquiry, experimentation and disconcerting honesty."[2]

---

[1] "In order to be recognised as legitimate process, restoration should not erase the traces of history," wrote Cesare Brandi, Italian specialist in conservation and restoration theory in his landmark theoretical essay on restoration, *Teoria del restauro*. "Restoration needs to acknowledge and respect the complex historical authenticity of the work of art and should not try to place itself outside of time [...] as a result of a human action, restoration therefore becomes a component of the work of art as passed on to the future." Therefore, all restoration work must be transparent and produce the appropriate documentation on the choices that have been made and the process that has been carried out, as well as reversible, allowing future restorers to trace back all the steps and even 'undo' what has been done.

A scene from *Titas Ekti Nadir Naam* (1973) **Courtesy:** Ritwik Memorial Trust

In selecting *Titas Ekti Nadir Naam* (1973) for restoration, urgency was a decisive factor. Ritaban Ghatak informed us that when the negative of *Titas* was discovered in Bangladesh in the late 1980s, 6 of the 17 reels of the camera negative and 3 of the sound negative were missing. At the time, a positive print in a good state of conservation was located and a dupe negative of the seven missing reels was made from it. Over the years, however, the print had decomposed and the dupe negative was all that was left. Whereas the original camera and sound negative were deposited at the NFAI, Ritaban had held on to the dupe negative at the Ritwik Memorial Trust in Kolkata. All the material—with the addition of a vintage print—was collected in Kolkata, and with the help of the Italian Consulate, shipped via diplomatic pouch to L'Immagine Ritrovata laboratory in Bologna.

The inspection of the original camera negative showed a slight instability, several damaged splices and numerous traces of mould. The main issue, however, seemed to be the presence of severe scratches that ran through the whole film. While some were quite thick and persistent through entire sequences, others were smaller but denser, covering the entire image for several frames. Since the intermediate material and the positive print were affected by an even higher number of scratches and flickering, besides presenting a considerable loss in detail and contrast, it was decided to search internationally for the missing reels. We found out that the Bundesarchiv-Filmarchiv had acquired the materials of the Staatliches Filmarchiv in erstwhile East Germany, among which was a first-generation combined lavender of *Titas Ekti Nadir Naam*, which was eventually used in combination with the negative during the restoration process. The Bundesarchiv-Filmarchiv also provided a second vintage print which was used, together with the one available at the NFAI, during the grading process.

Eliminating scratches was particularly problematic in all the heavy rain sequences as well as in the long shots with

[2] Jacob Levich, "Subcontinental Divide. The Undiscovered Art of Ritwik Ghatak" *Film Comment*, March/April 1997.

sudden changes of brightness and camera movements following the characters. The restoration focussed on stabilising and de-flickering the image, as well as correcting jumps on splices and density variations in cross-dissolves. Following physical repair, brushing clone tools were used to repair the splices while frame interpolation and extrapolation was applied for the most severely damaged. Automatic dirt removal was performed, besides manual removal of dirt and vertical scratches, followed by a quality check of artefacts. De-grain and de-noise correction was also carried out with the most damaged shots or to smooth the contrast between elements coming from different sources. The original opening credits were too damaged to be used: a great deal of care was applied in recreating them with the help of an Indian graphic designer, while Ritaban Ghatak helped identify shots in the film to replace the damaged footage used for the textless. Despite the poor condition of the available elements, their overall good photographic quality allowed for a very satisfactory result. *Titas Ekti Nadir Naam* received a very warm acclaim when premiered at the Cannes Film Festival in the spring of 2010 and was subsequently re-discovered in over 15 festivals worldwide. Following the restoration a new 35 mm internegative was produced.

Titas, negative, splice between negative film stock and dupe negative film stock
Image: L'Immagine Ritrovata

Special thanks to Davide Pozzi, Elena Tammaccaro and Marianna De Sanctis.

Cecilia Cenciarelli joined the Cineteca di Bologna in 2000 and has been working as project manager for Martin Scorsese's World Cinema Project since 2007.

SATYAJIT RAY'S APU TRILOGY
LEE KLINE

I work in a field made up of a very small but very passionate group. We love talking about film, resolution, restoration, picture formats, and digital tools. But most often, we tell everyone with any remote interest in the topic how much we love film. Why do we love it? Well, it's clearly because we like the way it looks. It's got grain. It's got movement. It's got stunning resolution. And one thing that all restoration people agree on: it can seemingly last forever.

Now I realise that this is potentially a surprising statement to make, because if you look at an actual piece of film, it appears very fragile and vulnerable. It can scratch easily and it can disintegrate if you don't take care of it. But if you do, it might very well be around for a long time. You can talk about digital lasting forever, and in theory it can, but how many digital formats have come and gone in our lifetime? The floppy disc? Try and play one of those. A firewire hard drive from 2004? Good luck getting that to work. How about a PCM audio tape? Do you know anyone who can play that back or even knows what it is?

If you look at some of the great archives in the world—

the British Film Institute, the Library of Congress, the Cinémathèque Française—you can find original film elements of movies that are over 100 years old stored in excellent conditions. That is pretty amazing. But film doesn't always last: throw in a little heat, add some moisture, or leave it near a window where the sun comes through, and 100 years can go down to 20 very quickly. Though if you store a hard drive or a videocassette in the same conditions, chances are you won't hold onto those much longer either.

To me, the most interesting thing about film is that in over 100 years it hasn't changed all that much. People have shot on 35 mm film for a very long time, and in some cases they still do. 16 mm film has been around since 1933. We can take the original negative of Fritz Lang's *M* from 1928, stored at the Berlin Bundesarchiv, and still pull beautiful images from it. And in 2015 we still have projectors, scanners, and lab equipment capable of playing back that same film! No one in the restoration world has to look at a reel of *M* and wonder, "What the heck is this thing?" Even a 15-year-old could likely look at a piece of film and know what it is. If you think about it, not many

Screenshot from *Pather Panchali* (1955) **Courtesy**: The Criterion Collection

man-made things last 100 years. Buildings do, and so do wines, but under the wrong circumstances these too may not last.

So, what does this all have to do with Satyajit Ray's Apu Trilogy? Quite a bit, actually. A couple of years ago I started doing research on the film assets for *Pather Panchali* (1955), *Aparajito* (1956), and *Apur Sansar* (1959). After years of negotiation, Criterion had secured the rights to all three films. We were excited to finally be able to include these seminal movies in our library. The first thing I typically do with all our films when we're ready to start working on them is to see what materials exist for each movie: negatives, prints, intermediate films, and soundtracks. With many films this research is relatively simple: you check with the owner and get an elements list. The list usually has all the assets for the films and you can pull in what you like from storage. But some films aren't as simple. This can be attributed to several factors, including changes of ownership, storage conditions, and most consistently, poor record-keeping. Sometimes in addition, elements are often shown as inventoried, but they're actually missing. Some elements are not usable

when you open the can because they have turned to vinegar. Sometimes a negative was lent out overseas and was never returned. I usually tell people I feel like a film detective, picking up clues from when the movie was released, sold, re-released, put on video, or simply locked somewhere in a warehouse.

Each country has preserved its films differently. For example, a studio in Hollywood had decided in the 1970s to 'eliminate' some original negatives because someone made the argument that making one reversal internegative (a low-contrast image used as the positive between an original camera negative and a duplicate negative) would satisfy the need for both protection and printing, and save on storage fees. Little did that someone know that these reversals would later fade on new, untested film stock from the era. Some Japanese studios made 16 mm dupes from their 35 mm nitrate originals to save on space and satisfy the 16 mm theatrical market. There have been some crazy archive practices all around the world, but it's not fair to blame any specific person or group in these cases. Decisions were made at a time when DVD, Blu-ray, streaming, and DCP were not even terms yet. Art-house cinemas showing small films were not considered to be big money-makers, and TV quality was limited to what people saw at the time. No one could have expected HD, 2K or 4K televisions.

When you finally find what you're looking for, the mystery of its quality comes into play. You nervously open the cans and check if they're complete and in good condition, or whether they've started disintegrating. Then comes the magic moment: a close inspection. This is typically done on a light table with a rewind setup and a magnifying viewer. Right away you can see if the film is stable, if it's scratched, if it's a dupe or an original, and, most importantly, if it's scannable or printable.

I remember a time when I had been searching for good film on Luis Buñuel's *Tristana* (1970). For years, we had looked for anything of good quality and had repeatedly come up empty. Our licensor had also been looking on our behalf, and one day I received a call informing me that some film had been located in a storage facility in England. It was thought to be a dupe. We had the film sent to the U.S., where the first inspection revealed that it was not a dupe at all, but actually the complete six reels of the original camera negative. But this was only partially good news: for some reason, the sixth and final reel of the negative was not in good shape. This reel had not only faded, but also had a completely different quality to it. We tried to do different tests to get something usable out of it, but whatever we tried would not reveal anything acceptable. Why this reel? What could have happened? I go into detective mode but I can never really find the answer. I'm not even sure how the negative got to England in the first place, or how it was stored for forty years.

And films don't have to be old to become lost. On Alfonso Cuarón's 2001 film *Y Tu Mama También*, we wanted to locate the original negative for a new scan. The film was owned by the same producer and distributed by the same company from the very beginning, but the negative was nowhere to be found. Two years went by before someone finally remembered that the negative was processed at Duart Labs in New York City. Duart was about to go out of business and close, and we were lucky to find the negative in their storage untouched since its initial use.

It's not always difficult though, and through the years we've found original negatives in excellent condition for dozens of films, including Alfred Hitchcock's *Foreign Correspondent* (1940), Luchino Visconti's 'Super Technirama' *The Leopard* (1963), Jules Dassin's *Rififi* (1955) and countless others. Sometimes just searching

for where these materials are located takes up most of your time, and then you find that they've been stored and unused since their original releases. And if you're in luck, stored well. Finding the right material for a restoration requires a great deal of detective work: it is actually half the job of being a restorer.

And that brings us back to the Apu Trilogy. Upon initial element evaluations for the three films, we kept finding mediocre dupes of each film, but never the original negative. The dupes were lacklustre; they were printed in poor conditions and had an insufficient gray scale. Criterion's sister company, Janus Films, had taken in some orphaned pre-print material many years back so we also had a few dupes (donated to the Harvard Film Archive) which merited evaluation. We also found that the archive at the Academy of Motion Picture Arts and Sciences in Los Angeles had some dupes they had restored back in the 1980s. I went to L.A. and started evaluating the Academy materials. But then something unexpected happened. Our friends at the Academy mentioned that a few reels of the original negative for *Aparajito* were preserved in deep storage in their vaults. They asked if I would want to have a look. Would I? Are you kidding? Yes, I would! Upon investigation, we found that eleven reels of the negative for *Aparajito* existed, as well as nine reels of *Pather Panchali* and two reels of *Apur Sansar*. But we're getting ahead of ourselves...

In July 1993, there was a fire at Hendersons Film Laboratories in South London. There's not a lot of information on the fire to be found; only a couple of articles in the local papers even make mention of it. It seems to have started in the nitrate film vaults and then spread to other parts of the vault. The fire was bad enough to damage many of the Ray films that had just arrived from India on their way to being preserved in Los Angeles. Luckily, even though they were badly burned, the Academy decided to have all the negatives shipped to L.A. and tucked them away in their vaults for the next 20 years.

I was at Sony Studios' top-notch postproduction facility Colorworks in Culver City doing some other work at the time, when the first of the burnt reels was delivered. I went down to the light table in the scanning area and had a look with one of Sony's excellent scanning technicians. We opened one of the cans and what we saw made us quickly step back. There was indeed a reel of film in the can, but it definitely looked like it had been in a fire. It was very warped, edges were frayed, heads were burned away, and the film was extremely brittle and flaking off.

We carefully took the best of the reels and slowly rewound it just enough to look between the sprockets. There was residue from tape and glue and wax throughout, but surprisingly, a decent image appeared to be lying in between the sprocket holes.

I had to see what kind of image we could get out of a scan, so I begged the scanning technician to scan at least a few seconds of the reel. And he did. Thank goodness for that, because what we saw was gorgeous. Due to the warping, the film was very unstable on the scanner and it was moving around quite a bit, but we got thirty seconds digitised. We then took the test back to Criterion to see what our digital tools could do, and, wouldn't you know it, we soon got some perfect images of *Aparajito*.

Encouraged, excited, and nervous, we then spent the next year trying to figure out how to work with this material. Because most of the great film technicians had either passed away or retired, this was no easy task. We spoke to dozens of people at labs all over the world, at Kodak, and at archives, and nobody could agree on the best way to handle burnt negatives. And how could they? No one we talked to had any firsthand experience of this kind of material, so what we got was mostly conjecture. "You can try this, but you can also try that" was often the response. To my mind, this was risky advice, because I knew that we would only get one shot at this, considering the fragile nature of the negatives. We needed an expert.

Burnt film and damaged sprockets in the negative of *Aparajito*.

With the help of the Academy, we set out to find the right people for the job. We had been doing a lot of work at L'Immagine Ritrovata in Bologna, Italy, for many years. We loved the passion and the expertise of the people there, and we valued their opinions. So we met them soon thereafter in Los Angeles to look at the negatives together. They had a clear plan: hydrate the film to make it less brittle, repair the splices, remove the glue and tape and wax, and fix all the sprockets. We could then do both pin-less and pin-registered scans in wet and dry gate and see what worked best (without the use of pins, the warped film could possibly move better through the gate on the scanner, but it would be less stable than using pin registration.) All this was music to my ears: it was clear that we had finally found someone with a plan that made sense. The folks at Bologna begged to do a test on a reel, and reel 3b of *Aparajito* was hand-carried back to Italy, where the repairs and tests then began.

Repaired sprockets of
Pather Panchali at Bologna

A few weeks later we received our first tests and realised that the only way to do this work correctly was to repair as much of the negative as possible and scan pin-registered wet gate. However, this approach was also the most costly. It meant hundreds of hours of repairs with skilled technicians, prior to any scanning, and then the use of wet-gate technology, which was slower and more expensive than conventional scanning (wet gate would help not only with the warping of the film, but it would also fill in any abnormalities like scratches, etc.). We partnered with the Academy to fund the project, and L'Immagine Ritrovato offered a substantial discount to take on the work. Without either partner, this project could never have gotten off the ground. The passion of these two collaborators to move the project forward was truly remarkable.

Images: The Criterion Collection

As the months went by, Bologna slowly repaired the negative. Some reels were beyond repair, and although others were repairable, it was still unclear

The restoration of *Apur Sansar*: A tear as well as a horizontal scratch are noticed. Using Digital Restoration Tools by Mathematical Technologies, we draw around the problem to help the computer identify what to fix. The restoration system uses frames before and after to fill in the damage with a clean image. Because the tear is so large, automated tools cannot work alone, so an operator is needed. A fix of this type can take about an hour assuming the frames before and after are usable. If they are warped or have density fluctuations, it could take several hours and the results may not be perfect.

Here is the same shot after the clean-up tools have been applied. A few scratches are left which can be quickly taken out.

A second frame near the first frame also has a tear that is in a different spot. Here we see the tear before the tools are applied.

The artist identifies the regions with the issues.

The fixed frame is complete and is checked while playing at 24 fps to make sure no artefacts remain.

Images: The Criterion Collection

if digital tools could correct some of the intense warping that happened from the heat of the fire. We would get updates every few weeks from the lab and decide how to proceed with the next batch. Once the material was repaired and scanned, it would then go to Criterion for the digital work. After a solid year of Bologna's dedication to tediously repairing and finally scanning the restored negative, more months and hundreds and hundreds of hours of digital repairs and colour grading would be added at Criterion.

Since the newly repaired negative was incomplete, we would need to find alternative film for missing sections or shots. Combing the world's archives for suitable replacements proved to be yet another challenge. Although the material from Janus and the Academy could work, we also found some fine grain positives and dupe negatives at the British Film Institute that were very good and would help a lot. Unfortunately, these were missing some shots and had black frames inserted at some point, so we needed to use the other dupes as alternatives to the alternatives. A complete assembly of the entire film was created in a digital timeline with an edit decision list identifying the best sections or shots of each film to be used. It was the roadmap that paved the way to the final restoration. Through the process, all aspects of scanning and digital restoration were kept in 4K resolution so that it would be at the highest affordable level possible. To do this work in anything but 4k (which is extremely close to full 35 mm film resolution) would have been a disservice to the restoration.

Besides the fact that only a certain number of reels were salvageable from the fire, each film had its own set of problems. *Pather Panchali*, the first film in the trilogy, was in the worst condition. The optically printed dissolves in the film were made crudely and quickly, and they were cut into the negative so they would snap out of the beautiful images surrounding them. Certain scenes in the negative were replaced by duplicate footage at some point in the film's lifetime, so they looked generationally inferior to other sections of the film. Wax was put on the surface of the entire negative to preserve it, but the fire had melted it into the picture. Luckily, wet-gate scanning helped this issue tremendously. Digital repairs at Criterion proved to be the most exhausting for this film, and even with months of additional work, the final product could not be made perfectly pristine. Only about 40% of the original negative could ultimately be used in the final version of the restoration, due to either missing footage, or extreme warping of the film which made the image unwatchable.

Aparajito had the most usable footage from the repaired and restored negatives. The replacement film for *Aparajito* was also in very good condition, so we ended up with a final version substantially better than the restored *Pather Panchali*. The filmmaking and editing of the film was also more advanced, so the optically printed shots for dissolves and fades were more sophisticated. We weren't as lucky with *Apur Sansar*. The two reels of negative that did survive were in the worst shape out of all the reels for the three films. The footage was so warped from the fire that repairs were deemed not worthwhile. The encouraging news was that the 35 mm fine grain that we ended up using (almost in its entirety) was extremely good. It was printed well and had an excellent gray scale, so the final result is exceptional even without access to the negative.

As I write this, Criterion is still deep in the trenches digitally repairing these films. Months have gone by just fixing scratches, tears, dirt, warping, flicker and instability, to name a few of the issues. Audio restorers are meticulously putting the final touches on the soundtracks bringing them up to contemporary digital standards. Some material looks and sounds great when it's restored, and some does not make out as well. Dupes used for missing negative footage have been inserted, but it's not like having the original, and we'll end up missing some great bits of picture information that the negative would have contained. But we're extremely lucky that some of the negatives for the Apu films were left intact. Ten years ago digital restoration techniques were not advanced enough to do much of this work, so timing was on our side. Back from the ashes, the Apu Trilogy lives on.

Lee Kline is Technical Director at the Criterion Collection, where he has headed the technical group for almost 20 years.

RESTORING SOUND FOR THE APU TRILOGY
RYAN HULLINGS

The sound restoration of the Apu Trilogy was an enormous undertaking. At Criterion, we strive to present film soundtracks as authentically as possible. Our processes aim to restore the sound to what it would have originally sounded like, almost as if you were hearing a pristine print in a great theatre the day the film was released. Integral to attaining this goal is the ability to differentiate between sounds that were recorded into the original soundtrack, and those that are the result of age and damage to an element. That distinction can be difficult at times, and we generally err on the side of authenticity by leaving potential imperfections alone, instead of removing something that may have always been part of the film and approved by its creators.

A good example of the complexity of this question: once, while restoring a Godard film, we happened to be working on a section of whispered voice-over that was rife with small clicks and pops that sounded a lot like surface noise on an optical track (dirt and dust on an optical track often produce a crackle similar to the sound of a beat-up vinyl record). Just as we were evaluating these sounds, a Godard scholar who was touring our offices stopped by. We played the VO for him, and he immediately knew what we were talking about. The scholar revealed that Godard had intentionally recorded that VO with a mic very close to his mouth to amplify the small clicks and pops people make naturally while speaking. Of course, we left the clicks and pops alone.

This sort of decision illustrates another important aspect of audio restoration. While tools that automatically remove clicks and pops are a vital part of audio postproduction and restoration, these automated processes often can't tell the difference between what's original and what's not. Only a person listening and fixing these small imperfections carefully by hand can make those decisions. It's a very time-consuming way to restore audio, but this method of working ultimately yields the most authentic results possible.

Just as it is with picture restoration, finding good original elements is paramount for getting good results. And just like the picture side of things, it wasn't easy for the Apu Trilogy. We evaluated elements from all over the world, most of which were so damaged as to be completely unusable. Some were exceptionally noisy, others heavily over-modulated and distorted. Both distortion and broadband noise are particularly difficult to fix without doing substantial damage to the underlying audio or introducing unacceptable artefacts, so these elements were of little use to us. Yet other elements had been previously processed with an aggressive bandpass filter that removes both high and low frequencies, similar to the 'Academy curve' filtering intended to standardise audio playback for theatres. This quickly removes a lot of what we hear as analog imperfections in sound, but it also makes tracks sound small and dark. Modern ears expect a wider frequency range from soundtracks than the Academy curve allows.

After lots of searching and listening, we collected what we believed to be the best audio available for the Trilogy. The best surviving sound element that we uncovered for *Pather Panchali* was a 35 mm magnetic track provided by the Academy. It's a safety master made at some point in the nineties after the fire. Though there is no record of exactly what element was used to make this mag, it was undoubtedly an optical element, as the mag track was full of surface noise, a signature of optical tracks. Each kind of audio element—mags, variable-area optical tracks, variable-density optical tracks, etc.—has certain audio imperfections that a natural result of the physical media used to store it. For instance, the dirt and dust that cause clicks and pops on

Screenshot from *Aparajito* (1956)
Courtesy: The Criterion Collection

optical tracks don't affect magnetic tracks in the same way. As such, there's really no surface noise on a mag: however, mags do often suffer from numerous dropouts and distortion, as well as wow and flutter (both of which are periodic pitch variations). As the *Pather Panchali* element was originally an optical track that was transferred to a mag, the defects were compounded, and we had to fix problems from both sources. Working primarily in Pro Tools and using various digital tools, we manually removed the vestiges of age (clicks, pops, crackle, thumps, hiss, hum, distortion, dropouts ... the list goes on), shaped the timbre of the soundtrack using EQs, and tightly synchronised sound with picture. I'm proud of the results we were able to obtain, and I believe the film must sound better now than at any time since the day of its release. The issue of authenticity was particularly important for this film, as its audio editing can sound a bit crude at times. We intentionally didn't smooth out the occasional abrupt change in room tone or dialogue quality resulting from the overdubbing of a line or a coarse audio edit. These aspects of the soundtrack are important parts of the history of the film and provide insight into just how it was constructed.

Of the three films in the trilogy, suitable audio sources for *Apur Sansar* were the most difficult to come by. Again, we found good sources at the Academy, but the best-sounding source, a 35 mm print, was incomplete. We transferred this print and used it for much of the film, but several reels from a second, slightly inferior print were used to fill the gaps. We then conformed all of this audio to our picture master and discovered that we were still missing some material. Both of our 35 mm prints had been truncated at reel boundaries, so we had to find yet another source to fill in those gaps. Fortunately, the Academy had another 35 mm mag that contained the missing reel transitions. But unfortunately, this mag had been previously been (lightly) restored, so it sounded very different from our nice prints. The mag wasn't full-bandwidth—someone had applied something like the Academy curve I mentioned previously, making the track sound small and old. We set to matching these three sources using advanced EQs and mastering techniques in Pro Tools, and now the transitions between the reels are complete and seamless. The prints required an exceptional number of manual fixes to remove surface noise. Though the underlying audio sounded very good, the prints were dirty and there were many layers of grit between the listener and the original soundtrack recording. More than a month of intensive audio restoration has yielded exciting results, but as I write this, we're not quite finished. Though it can be maddening, there's almost always another minuscule pop or click to fix.

We will soon begin the restoration of *Aparajito*. We were lucky to turn up a very nice-sounding complete 35 mm print in Italy that was transferred in Bologna. It conformed easily to match our picture master, which was a welcome relief after *Apur Sansar*. The print is still quite dirty, and, like *Apur Sansar*, it will require extensive digital restoration over the next month or so. Loud dialogue and SFX on this element are quite distorted, but my preliminary tests indicate that we'll be able to dramatically improve these problems. I'm excited to begin work and to hear just how good it can sound.

Ryan Hullings is supervisor of the audio department at the Criterion Collection.

THE FILM HERITAGE 60

A REPORT BY THE FILM HERITAGE FOUNDATION

THE FILM HERITAGE **60**

A BEGINNING FOR FILM RESTORATION IN INDIA

On the sets of *Sant Tukaram* (1936)

The Film Heritage Foundation was conceived with a single goal—to save India's cinematic heritage. When we started out in January 2014, we were aware that the task we had set ourselves was daunting, especially our ambitious plan to help preserve and restore India's film classics. We had a million ideas on what needed to be done, but soon enough, the questions began to crop up: Where to begin? Which films to take up first? And in no time, there were even more troubling questions: Where do we find these films anyway? What survives of our classics, what condition are they in? How can we save them? Is it already too late?

The Film Heritage 60 is our attempt to find answers to these questions, as a beginning for film restoration in India. In consultation with P. K. Nair, India's foremost archivist and a former director of the NFAI, we drew up a longlist of films that we believed represented the core of India's film heritage. Next, we set about investigating what material was available for these films, and its current condition: based on this research, we drew up the report presented in the following pages. This is by no means a definitive list of Indian classics, or a canon of any kind: these are, quite simply, endangered films for which we thankfully do have surviving material that can be restored. These are the films that *can* and *must* be brought back to life. The next step for our foundation will be to collaborate with the copyright-holders, the government, the film industry, and the public in general to work towards restoring these films. We need to come together to save them before it is too late, and even the surviving material is lost forever.

When we set out to make the list, it was difficult to determine where to begin and what parameters to use in the selection, given that our country has one of the most prolific and diverse film industries in the world. We decided to focus on a time frame from the beginning of the talkies up to the 1960s. There are of course many worthy films that have come before and after, but it is this period, we believe, which is the most critical one, where immediate attention is required. The films of the silent era we excluded with the understanding that every surviving Indian silent film—from Phalke's *Raja Harishchandra* (1913), India's first feature film, to *Ghulami Nu Patan* (1931)—deserves to be restored, just by dint of its rarity. (This includes the 1919 film *Bilwamangal*, the original nitrate negative of which was recently sighted at the Cinémathèque Française in Paris).

Even within this limited time frame, it was hard work whittling down our longlist to just 60 films. At the outset, we left out Satyajit Ray's films and others which have already been taken up for restoration with the help of the international film community. Choosing from the rest made for some difficult decisions: just as an example, we managed to include *Achchut Kanya* (1936) in the list, but not other notable Bombay Talkies' films such as *Jawaani ki Hawa* (1935) and *Bandhan* (1940), and we were compelled also to leave out important films such as *Khandaan* (1942), *Roti* (1942), *Ratan* (1944), *Gopinath* (1948), *Barsaat* (1949), and *Bandini* (1963). While we tried our best to represent the regional cinemas of India, there were unavoidable omissions such as *Pavalakkodi* (1934), *Swarga Seema* (1945) and S. S. Vasan's *Avvaiyar* (1953) from the south; *President* (1937) and *Kapalkundala* (1939) from the Bengali cinema; *Sant Dnyaneshwar* (1940) and *Ram Shastri* (1944) in Marathi; and *Chaman* (1948), the first Punjabi film. These are a few examples; there are numerous other films which deserve a place here.

In the end, we selected the titles that we considered landmarks in our film history, important films that also reflected the spirit of their times. The condition of the available material was another important criterion for selection; some films, we discovered, were in a precarious state, hanging by a thread. We were shocked to learn that for well-known films like P. C. Barua's Bengali version of *Mukti* (1937) and Ellis Dungan's *Sakuntalai* (1940), there was only one surviving print. For *Kaagaz ke Phool* (1959), India's first Cinemascope film, there was only one surviving vintage print in the original Cinemascope format. Even for some later films like Ramu Kariat's *Mudiyanaya Puthran* (1961) and the Bengali film *Saptapadi* (1961), only one print could be traced. Of Bimal Roy's *Naukri*

(1954), nothing survives on 35 mm: all that is left is a 16 mm print. For all these films, no original camera negative or dupe negative survives. What we have instead are prints intended for projection, which typically have a life of 250 to 300 screenings: from their poor condition, it is evident that they have been screened many, many times, and are literally fading away.

In our research, we looked primarily for material surviving on celluloid. Many of the films on the list are black-and-white films shot originally on nitrate. At the time they were shot, every single print in circulation was struck directly from the original camera negative. When duplication stock became available, filmmakers were advised to take out dupe negatives or master positives from the original camera negatives, using them as high-quality backups in case the original camera negative was damaged or destroyed. However, Indian producers rarely took the trouble to make dupe negatives or master positives from the original camera negative. Tragically, they did not even bother to preserve the original camera negatives (OCN), which are the highest quality source one needs to make the best copies. Even for films as recent as Mansoor Khan's *Qayamat Se Qayamat Tak* (1988), Mani Ratnam's *Thalapathi* (1991) and Sanjay Leela Bhansali's *Khamoshi* (1996), there is no trace of the OCNs. In their absence, copies were made using the next available generation of material, with the inevitable loss of quality. We found that for almost all the titles here, the available sources were rather unsatisfactory.

Some titles were included in our longlist because we assumed that prints at least would be available. Sadly, we were wrong. Mr Nair insisted on including C. V. Sridhar's *Kalyana Parisu* (1959), because he remembered material surviving in Chennai: however, we could not find any trace of this film, and are still looking for it. Gulzar *saheb* recommended including *Kabuliwala* (1961) in the list, but we discovered that nothing remains of this film. A great deal was lost with the introduction of U-matic and Betacam technologies, when copyright-holders and producers transferred their films to tape, failing to realise that they still needed to preserve their OCNs, master positives and dupe negatives. Several important films now survive only in inferior video copies. For instance, we recently discovered a clip of Kidar Sharma's *Neelkamal* (1947), Raj Kapoor and Madhubala's debut film, on the internet. While this would have been an obvious addition to our list, we discovered that it was uploaded from a U-matic copy, and neither the original source material nor the U-matic for that matter could be traced. The cinephiles and film-industry veterans we consulted for our list were often surprised to learn that if a film was available on DVD or YouTube, this did not necessarily mean that the film had been preserved and was available for restoration.

The message is clear: if you do not preserve the original source material, there will be nothing left to restore. India's cinematic heritage should not become a graveyard of memories: images on the silver screen that made audiences laugh and cry, only to fade away like ghosts. Cinema is an art, a form of creative expression, as well as an invaluable visual history of the times we live in. We need to save and restore the surviving remnants of its past, and ensure that we preserve its present too for the future.

Glossary of terms

Original camera negative (OCN) is the original source of any film. This is the film element that is exposed in the camera and records the footage while shooting.

Master positive or Fine grain master refers mostly to black-and-white film stock. It is an intermediate element bearing positive images on negative stock. It is the intermediate step between an OCN and a duplicate negative. It cannot be used for projection.

Duplicate negative or dupe negative refers mostly to black-and-white film stock. It is a copy of the negative as close as possible to the original. It can derive from a fine grain master or a print. The dupe negative can combine both picture and sound, but most often the sound negative is separate.

Release print is the positive element used for theatrical projection.

Intermediate film is any duplicate element between a camera original and a print. It can bear positive or negative images, and can be used to create prints or other duplicate elements. It cannot be used for projection.

Internegative refers to duplicate colour film stock. It is a colour negative made from a colour print or reversal camera original. It can be used to create an interpositive or a print.

Interpositive or intermediate positive refers to duplicate colour film stock. It is an intermediate element bearing positive images. It can be created from an OCN or another intermediate element.

Intermediate negative refers to duplicate colour film stock. It is a negative made from an interpositive.

Amrit Manthan

back, side-stepped and lost our way [From *Filmindia*, July 1935].

02 AMRIT MANTHAN

1934, Marathi | B&W, 155 minutes
Director: V. Shantaram **Producer**: Prabhat Film Company **Story**: Based on Narayan Hari Apte's novel Bhagyashree **Cinematographer**: Keshavrao Dhaiber **Music**: Keshavrao Bhole **Cast**: Keshavrao Date, Nalini Tarkhad, Shanta Apte, Sureshbabu Mane, Kelkar, Kulkarni, Budasaheb, Desai.

V. Shantaram's film opens with a sinister cabal plotting regicide against a king who has banned the ritual sacrifice of human beings and animals. Deftly balancing intricately plotted palace intrigue with social reformist themes that are still relevant today, *Amrit Manthan* was a technical watershed for Indian cinema, and Prabhat's first all-India hit.

Available Material: The original camera negative does not survive. It was lost in the nitrate fire at the FTII in Pune in January 2003.
NFAI: 2 master positives (35 mm), one of 17 reels, one of 15 reels; 2 release positives (35 mm), one of 17 reels, one of 15 reels.

Ashish Rajadhyaksha on *Amrit Manthan*
    The first really big blockbuster released by the Prabhat Film Company after the coming of sound, this is also V. Shantaram announcing his expressionist signature style. The film begins with a sensational low-angle circular track movement as the cult followers of the demoness Chandika meet in a dungeon of flickering lights and deep shadow, and plot to kill the good king.
    The elaborately constructed film has several famous scenes including the twice-told legend of the churning of the seas, once by the priest to show how evil must be exorcised, and again by a good general to show how demons often appear disguised as gods. Shantaram, it was said, had used several techniques he claimed to have received from German expressionism, including the systematic recourse to artificial light, even bleaching the film in places, and, in the film's most famous shot, the telephoto lens focussed on the priest's right eye in his opening declaration.

01 CHANDIDAS

1932, Bengali | B&W, 133 minutes
Director: Debaki Kumar Bose **Producer**: New Theatres **Cinematographer**: Nitin Bose **Music**: Raichand Boral **Cast**: Durgadas Banerjee, K.C. Dey, Amar Mullick, Uma Sashi, Manoranjan Bhattacharya, Dhirendra Bandopadhyay, Chani Dutta, Sunila.

Chandidas established the Kolkata-based New Theatres as one of the most prominent studios in the country and its director Debaki Kumar Bose as a filmmaker with a uniquely personal vision. Adapted from a popular stage musical, the film is about Chandidas (Banerjee), a little-known Vaishnavite poet from medieval Bengal, and his relationship with a washer-woman (Uma Sashi), which invites the malicious attention of an influential merchant of high status. The film adaptation focussed on Chandidas'

poetry, which decries forms of institutionalised religion that sanction social inequality, invoking a more egalitarian and just god.

Available Material: The original camera negative was lost in a nitrate fire at the film storage vaults of New Theatres, Tollygunge in August 1940.
NFAI: 1 master positive (35 mm), 12 reels; 1 release positive (35 mm) 12 reels, not in a good condition. **George Eastman House, USA:** 16 mm acetate release positive, 3 reels.

Baburao Patel on *Chandidas*
    I remember *Chandidas*. It was almost lyrical. When all the films are melted down to yield silver, let us preserve *Chandidas* for posterity, not because it made film history, but because it failed to do so. It was a turning point in Indian films but we turned

Achhut Kanya

03 ACHHUT KANYA

1936, Hindi | B&W, 136 minutes
Director: Franz Osten **Producer**: Himanshu Rai
(Bombay Talkies) **Story**: Niranjan Pal **Dialogue,
Lyrics**: J.S. Casshyap **Cinematographer**: Josef
Wirsching **Music**: Saraswati Devi **Cast**: Ashok
Kumar, Devika Rani, P.F. Pithawala, Kamta Prasad,
Kishori Lal, Kusum Kumari, Pramila, Anwar, Ishrat.

The first formal offering from Bombay
Talkies, *Achhut Kanya* broke social
taboos when it dared to show a Brahmin
boy and an untouchable girl in love with
each other, as well as society's violent
opposition to their romance. The film's
success sparked off the trend of making
socially conscious films set in contemporary times. The production brought
together the talents of one of the most
cohesive technical teams of the period:
director Franz Osten, cinematographer Josef Wirsching, and screenwriters
Niranjan Pal and J. S. Casshyap.

Available Material: Shot originally on
nitrate stock, processed at the Bombay
Talkies lab in Malad, the original camera
negative does not survive.
NFAI: 1 master positive, 15 reels, processed at the Famous Cine Lab, Tardeo;
1 dupe negative, 15 reels; 4 release positives, 15 reels; all on 35 mm

04 AMAR JYOTI

1936, Hindi | B&W, 166 minutes
Director: V. Shantaram **Producer**: Prabhat Film
Company **Screenplay**: K. Narayan Kale **Dialogue,
Lyrics**: Narottam Vyas **Cinematographer**: V.
Avadhoot **Music**: Master Krishnarao **Cast**: Durga
Khote, Shanta Apte, Chandra Mohan, K. Narayan
Kale, B. Nandrekar, Vasanti, K. Narayan Kale,
Vasanti, Aruna.

Amar Jyoti can lay legitimate claim to
being a proto-feminist film with its central character of a mother who turns
into a pirate when denied legal custody
of her child. Durga Khote's Saudamini,
the scorned mother, declares an all-
out war against the patriarchal laws of
the land and especially against the mor-

Amar Jyoti

ally depraved minister Durjaya, played
by Chandramohan. This was the first
Prabhat production to blend the studio's
regular offering of reformist themes with
popular elements such as the considerable swordplay and stunt-work seen in
the film.

Available Material: The original camera
negative was lost in the fire at FTII, Pune
in January 2003.
NFAI: 1 master positive; 1 release positive; 1 dupe negative; 15 reels each, all on
35 mm

05 DEVDAS

1936, Hindi | B&W, 141 minutes
Director: Pramathesh Chandra Barua **Producer**:
New Theatres **Story**: Based on Sarat Chandra
Chattopadhyay's novel *Devdas*. **Cinematographer**:
Bimal Roy **Dialogue, Lyrics**: Kidar Sharma **Music**:
Raichand Boral, Pankaj Mullick **Cast**: Kundan Lal
Saigal, Jamuna, Pahadi Sanyal, K.C. Dey, Rajkumari,
Kshetrabala, Kidar Sharma, A.H. Shorey, Biswanath
Bhaduri, Nemo, Ramkumari, Bikram Kapoor.

K. L. Saigal played the weak-willed, tor-
tured alcoholic lead character in the film,
and put in a definitive performance that
has made the name 'Devdas' a synonym
for the self-destructive lover. The film
was notable for featuring the early work
of two important filmmakers: Bimal Roy
as cinematographer and Kidar Sharma as
dialogue writer and lyricist. Roy's work,
especially, was considered groundbreaking, with his restless camera movements
and his use of camera filters to convey different psychological states of characters.
Sharma's songs for Saigal such as *'Dukh
ke din ab beetat nahin'* have inspired
many over the years.

Available Material: The original camera
negative was lost in the nitrate fire at
New Theatres, Kolkata, in 1940. Years
later, New Theatres handed over all the
film material it had to the NFAI. Today,
the master positive on 35 mm has decomposed. The only surviving print of the
Bengali version (starring P. C. Barua) is
with the Bangladesh Film Archive.
NFAI: 1 master positive (35 mm) 13 reels,
decomposed; 1 sound negative, not in
a great condition; 1 release positive (35
mm), 13 reels, lots of scratches.

Basu Chatterjee on *Devdas*

My dream is to watch the restored *Devdas* one day. *Devdas* was a trendsetter and a landmark film that should always be preserved in our film history. When it was released, it was really a big thing because it showed a young man breaking social traditions to live by his idealism. P. C. Barua's 1936 film was one of the first made on the novel *Devdas* written by Sarat Chandra, and it inspired the many versions that came after it. The story was relevant then and continues to be relevant now.

06 SANT TUKARAM

1936, Marathi | B&W, 131 minutes
Director: Vishnupant Damle, Sheikh Fattelal
Producer: Prabhat Film Company **Story**:
Shivram Vashikar **Lyrics**: Shantaram Athavale
Cinematographer: V. Avadhoot **Music**: Keshavrao Bhole **Cast**: Vishnupant Pagnis, Gauri, B. Nandrekar, Shankar Kulkarni, Bhagwat, Kusum Bhagwat, Shanta Majumdar, Master Chhotu, Pandit Damle.

Based on the life of a revered saint, *Sant Tukaram* nonetheless steers clear of hagiography and remains firmly rooted in the real and the everyday. The performances and set design are in consonance with this down-to-earth approach to the material, with Gauri's earthy rendition of Jijai particularly resonant with audiences till date. Even the numerous miracles shown in the film are endowed with a quiet credence. The film ran in theatres continuously for over a year, in addition to being adjudged one of the three best films in the world at the 1937 Venice International Film Festival.

Available Material: The original camera negative does not exist. It was lost in the fire at FTII, Pune in January 2003. Apart from the material with the NFAI, the British Film Institute has a print of *Sant Tukaram*, which they exchanged for a print of Hitchcock's *Blackmail* with the NFAI in the 1960s.
NFAI: 1 master positive (35 mm) 17 reels; 1 combined dupe negative (35 mm),15 reels; 8 release positives (35 mm), 15 reels; five 16 mm prints. **British Film Institute (BFI)**: 1 print on safety film, 15 reels, 12328 ft. in length, without end titles, oil and dirt, scratched cue dots, and

previous repairs. **George Eastman House, USA**: 16 mm release positive, 4 reels.

Kumar Shahani on *Sant Tukaram*

Sant Tukaram is a film of extraordinary performances, displaying tremendous freedom in combining styles—from the *abhinaya* of the classical to the manneristic postures of Ravi Varma's paintings to the realistic caricatures of the newly emerging popular culture. It is made with such conviction in the poetry of the great saint that all its naïveté turns into a form of transcendental wisdom.

Govind Nihalani on *Sant Tukaram*

Sant Tukaram is an outstanding achievement in creating a unique cinematic experience. It is one of those rare films in which history, myth and miracle are so seam-

lessly integrated that the entire film feels 'real'. It is amazing to see how the dialogue flows into an *abhang* and history metamorphoses into miracle. It is a film that defies any genre... in fact, if at all, the term 'magic realism' could be applied to any film, *Sant Tukaram* would perhaps be the first and most eminently deserving one. And it was made decades before the world had even heard of the term.

07 CHINTAMANI

1937, Tamil | B&W, 215 minutes
Director: K. Subrahmanyan **Producer**: Royal Talkies **Screenplay**: Y.V. Rao **Dialogue**: Somyajulu, Serugalathur Sama **Cinematography**: B. Washgar **Music**: Papanasam Sivan **Cast**: M.K. Thyagaraja Bhagavathar, Papanasam Sivan, L. Narayan Rao, Y.V. Rao, Ashwathamma, Serugalathur Sama.

Sant Tukaram

A morality tale about the redemptive power of devotion, *Chintamani* is based on the tale of the legendary devotee of Lord Krishna, Bilwamangal of Varanasi and his infatuation with the courtesan Chintamani, herself a passionate Krishna devotee. The first Tamil adaptation of the story (it had been made in Hindi, Telugu, Bengali previously), it was a huge success, running in cinema halls continuously for over a year. It featured breakthrough performances by legendary Tamil actor M.K. Thyagaraja Bhagavathar and Ashwathamma, as well as an enduringly popular soundtrack.

Available Material: The original camera negative does not exist. The only surviving material is preserved at the NFAI.

NFAI: 1 combined dupe negative; 1 sound negative; 1 release positive; 19 reels each, all on 35 mm.

---

08 KUNKU

1937, Marathi | B&W, 162 minutes
Director: V. Shantaram **Producer**: Prabhat Film Company **Story**: Based on Narayan Hari Apte's novel *Na Patnari Goshta* **Cinematographer**: V. Avadhoot **Lyrics**: Shantaram Athavale **Music**: Keshavrao Bhole **Cast**: Shanta Apte, Keshavrao Date, Raja Nene, Shakuntala Paranjpye, Vimala Vashishth, Vasanti, Gauri, Master Chhotu, Karmarkar.

Like the novel on which it is based, *Kunku* is a landmark in the women's movement in Maharashtra, stridently denouncing the practice of forcing women into marriage without their consent or any regard for their rights. The narrative's central character Neera, played by Shanta Apte, is trapped into marrying a widower, a fairly progressive lawyer with children nearly her own age. She refuses to accept her marital status, and in an ultimate gesture of defiance, wipes off the red bindi mark on her forehead—the symbol of marital commitment.

Available Material: Both the Marathi version of this film as well as its Hindi version *Duniya Na Mane* are preserved at the NFAI.
NFAI: 1 master positive, 16 reels; 1 release positive, 15 reels; both on 35 mm.

Sumitra Bhave on *Kunku*

Kunku has a very special place in the history of Indian cinema because it is the first film which strongly upholds a woman's right to dignity and decision-making with astonishing intellectual clarity. The film goes uncompromisingly to the logical extreme of depicting an old widower committing suicide, moved by the protests of his new bride who is younger than his own daughter. The daughter, a reformist and a rebel herself, is on the side of her stepmother and openly condemns her father.

Kunku, once deemed 'an unacceptable story', is certainly a treasure to be preserved—for its cinematic experimentation and its innovative sound design; and also for its depiction of the cultural history of India in the twenties and thirties.

Sai Paranjpye on *Kunku*

Made under the Prabhat Chitra banner by V. Shantaram in 1937, *Kunku* was a highly committed social film, well ahead of its time. Apart from a very bold theme, the film was deftly directed, and all the credible characters were beautifully portrayed. (I am tempted to mention here that my mother Shakuntala Paranjpye, herself a renowned social worker, played the important role of Chitra, the heroine's young step-mother).

Kunku is a cinematic gem. A truly great film to remember and cherish, and above all, to preserve lovingly.

Kamal Haasan on *Kunku*

I discovered this film after I finished four filmed screenplays. It humbled me enough to go back to school. I did not give any concession to the filmmaker for being half a century behind me. He was ahead by nearly that much in skill and honesty.

09 MUKTI

1937, Bengali | B&W, 139 min
Director: P. C. Barua **Producer**: New Theatres **Cinematographer**: Bimal Roy **Screenplay**: P.C. Barua **Story**: Sajanikanta Das **Dialogue**: Sajanikanta Das **Lyrics**: Sajanikanta Das, Rabindranath Tagore, Ajoy Bhattacharya **Cast**: P.C. Barua, Kanan Devi, Menaka, Amar Mullick, Pankaj Mullick, Sailen Choudhury, Ahi Sanyal, Indu Mukherjee.

Mukti follows the trajectories of a married couple Prasanta (Barua) and Chitra (Kanan Devi). He is an artist in the romantic tradition, obsessed with his work and least bothered about social propriety (he paints nudes), much to the chagrin of his conservative father-in-law. Though Prasanta and Chitra are in love, both are unwilling to compromise on their ideals and decide to separate. Through a convoluted series of events they meet again, under vastly different circumstances. *Mukti* was the first major instance of Tagore's songs being used for the soundtrack of a film.

Available Material: The original camera negative and the dupe negative of this film do not survive.
NFAI: **Bengali version**: 1 release positive, 14 reels, not in a great condition. **Hindi version**: 1 master positive, 13 reels, not in good condition; 1 release positive, 13 reels, in comparatively better condition.

10 VIDYAPATI

1937, Hindi | B&W, 152 minutes
Director: Debaki Kumar Bose **Producer**: New Theatres **Screenplay**: Debaki Kumar Bose, Kazi Nazrul Islam **Cinematographer**: Yusuf Mulji **Lyrics**: Kidar Sharma **Cast**: Pahadi Sanyal, Prithviraj Kapoor, Kanan Devi, Chhaya Devi, K. C. Dey, Lila Desai, K. N. Singh, Nemo, Kidar Sharma, Rampiyari, Mohammed Ishaq.

Set in the court of Mithila's King Shiva Singha (Kapoor), *Vidyapati* follows the romantic upheavals in the lives of the royal couple upon the arrival of the poet Vidyapati (Sanyal). Kanan Devi, playing

the role of the poet's faithful follower Anuradha, delivered a landmark intense performance. Vidyapati's verse was central to the film's narrative, with the poet's stirring recitals presented in sustained close-ups. The film eschewed the static frontal compositions that had been *de rigueur* for devotional films until then for a more fluid visual style.

Available Material: The original camera negative of this film does not survive. In 1970, New Theatres deposited a 35 mm print of 14 reels at the NFAI.
NFAI: 1 master positive, 13 reels; 1 dupe negative, 14 reels (with only picture and no sound); 1 release positive, 13 reels, lots of scratches; all on 35 mm.

11 MANOOS

1939, Marathi | B&W, 160 minutes
Director: V. Shantaram **Producer**: Prabhat Film Company **Cinematographer**: V. Avadhoot **Story**: A. Bhaskarrao **Screenplay**: Anant Kanekar **Dialogue, Lyrics**: Anant Kanekar **Music**: Master Krishnarao **Cast**: Shahu Modak, Shanta Hublikar, Sundarabai, Raja Paranjpe, Ram Marathe, Budasaheb, Gauri, Manju, Narmada, Ganpatrao, Manajirao.

Manoos tells the tragic story of the upright police officer Ganpat (Modak) and the prostitute Maina (Hublikar). Though they are in love with each other, Maina never overcomes her guilt about her social status and resists his attempts to rehabilitate her. Shot almost entirely on sets that faithfully recreated the shadowy, deserted alleyways of Mumbai, Shantaram uses expressionist techniques to a greater extent and effect than before. The film is notable for having the first multi-lingual song in Indian cinema, rendered and enacted by Shanta Hublikar in seven languages.

Available Material: Originally shot on nitrate, the original camera negative does not survive. It was lost in the nitrate fire at FTII, Pune in January 2003.
NFAI: 1 master positive, 15 reels; 2 release positives, 15 reels each; all on 35 mm.

12 PUKAR

1939, Urdu | B&W, 151 minutes
Director: Sohrab Modi **Producer**: Minerva Movietone **Cinematographer**: Y.D. Sarpotdar **Story, Lyrics**: Kamal Amrohi **Music**: Mir Saheb **Cast**: Sohrab Modi, Chandra Mohan, Naseem Banu, Sardar Akhtar, Sadiq Ali, Sheela

Vidyapati

Pukar was the first of the big-budget epics produced by Sohrab Modi and his Minerva studio. Set in the Mughal period, the film deals with the justice meted out by the Emperor Jehangir (Chandramohan). Kamal Amrohi's script presents two stories: the romance between lovers Mangal Singh and Kanwar, whose families are at war with each other, and the story of the Queen Nurjehan (Banu), Jehangir's own consort, who is accused by a washerwoman of inadvertently killing her husband while on a hunt. Jehangir's personal code of uniform justice across classes is put to the gravest test as the two dilemmas threaten to influence each other. The film features some of the most lavish scenes of royal grandeur in Indian cinema.

Available Material: Originally processed at the Bombay Film Laboratories Pvt. Ltd., the only surviving material of the film is preserved at the NFAI.
NFAI: 1 master positive, 15 reels; 1 combined dupe negative, 15 reels, processed at the FTII lab; 1 sound negative, 15 reels; 5 release positives, 15 reels; all on 35 mm.

Jaya Bachchan on *Pukar*

If we can speak of preservation, of preserving our culture, our music, dance and art, then why not cinema? Cinema *is* an art! It is dynamic, as visually dynamic as sculpture, as our temples, it is as alive as the Khajuraho temple. We must preserve it for the generations to come.

I remember Sohrab Modi's *Pukar*, a film that spoke of justice and fairness above all, a film of high drama written by Kamal Amrohi. It had eloquent Urdu dialogues that inspired many films that followed. I remember the powerful performances of Chandramohan in the role of Jehangir, and the towering Sohrab Modi as Sangram Singh.

13 RAITHU BIDDA

1939, Telugu | B&W, 175 minutes
Director: Gudavalli Ramabrahmam **Producer:** Sri Sarathi Studios **Cinematography:** Sailen Bose **Dialogue:** T. Gopichand **Lyrics:** Kosaraju, Tapi Dharma Rao, Basavaraju Apparao, Nellore Venkatarama Naidu, Tummala Seetarama Murthy Choudhury **Music:** B. Narasimha Rao **Cast:** Bellari

Diamond Queen

Raghava, G.V. Sitapati, Tanguturi Suryakumari, S. Varalakshmi, B. Narsimha Rao, Suribabu, M.C. Raghavan, Nellore Nagaraja Rao

The fact that land-owning feudal groups and sections of the royalty in Madras Presidency vociferously objected to the film's release, going so far as to burn copies of its print publicly and eventually banning it in Nellore and Chennai, testifies to its commitment to land and labour reforms. A reformist melodrama, the film follows a minor landowner Narsi Reddy (Raghavan) who is humiliated publicly when he chooses to vote for a peasant candidate against a landlord-backed political party. The film is an exploration of the various nexuses between the landholding elite, the police and politicians. The film is at its most trenchantly political in its militant songs, written by Andhra Pradesh Kisan Sabha activist N. Venkatrama Naidu.

Available Material: The original camera negative does not survive and there is no dupe negative either.
NFAI: 1 master positive, 19 reels; 4 release positives, 19 reels; all on 35 mm.

14 THYAGABHOOMI

1939, Tamil | B&W, 194 minutes
Director: K. Subrahmanyam **Producer:** Madras United Artists Corporation, K. Subramanyam **Cinematographer:** Sailen Bose **Story:** R. Krishnamurthy (Kalki) **Screenplay:** K. Subrahmanyam **Music:** Papanasam Sivan, Moti

Babu **Cast**: S.D. Subbulaksmi, Papanasam Sivan, Baby Saroja, A.K. Kamalam, K.J. Mahadevan.

The biggest hit from the Tamil cinema of the 30's, *Thyagabhoomi* is a film intensely involved in the issues of the times. Propelled by reformist Gandhian ideals, it invokes the campaign against untouchability and the temple-entry movement in the state. The plot deals with Sastry (Sivan), a *charkha*-spinning brahmin priest, who provides shelter to Harijans in the village temple, for which he is banished from the village. A parallel track concerns his daughter Savitri's struggles against a patriarchal society, resolved when her evil husband becomes a nationalist.

Available Material: The film's nationalist message led to it being banned six weeks after its release in 1939 by the British. The original camera negative and the prints were seized by the police and later surfaced at the Bombay Film Laboratories Pvt. Ltd. in 1963. After that, there is no record of the original camera negative. No material survives of this blockbuster anywhere in India, except for whatever has been preserved at the NFAI.
NFAI: 1 master positive, 20 reels; 1 release positive, 20 reels, with many scratches; both on 35 mm.

Theodore Bhaskaran on *Thyagabhoomi*

A fine example of the patriotic cinema of the thirties, *Thyagabhoomi* touched upon Gandhian programs of temple entry, anti-untouchability and temperance. The film established its credibility by conforming to basic Indian beliefs even as it questioned social evils. The main protagonist was made to resemble Gandhi, and this device added to the impact of this milestone film of Tamil cinema.

15 DIAMOND QUEEN

1940, Hindi | B&W, 155 minutes
Director: Homi Wadia **Producer**: Wadia Movietone **Cinematographer**: R.P. Master **Story**: J.B.H. Wadia **Dialogue, Lyrics**: Munshi Shyam **Music**: Madhavlal D. Master **Cast**: Nadia, John Cawas, Radha Rani, Boman Shroff, Sardar Mansoor, Sayani, Nazira, Dalpat, Kunjru, Minoo the Mystic.

While *Hunterwali* and *Miss Frontier Mail* established 'Fearless' Nadia's screen persona as the righteous daredevil singlehandedly taking on thugs, *Diamond Queen* used the archetype to address explicitly social concerns. Returning after three years in Mumbai to her ancestral village, Madhurika (Nadia) finds it under the grip of a dastardly villain involved in all sorts of nefarious activities. With the aid of her trusted horse, a magical car and a reformed dacoit Diler (Cawas), Madhurika cleans up the village.

The film featured extensive stunt-work and showed off Nadia's swashbuckling swordplay.

Available Material:
NFAI: 1 combined dupe negative, 13 reels; 2 release positives, 15 reels and 13 reels; all on 35 mm.

16 SAKUNTALAI

1940, Tamil | B&W, 180 minutes
Director: Ellis Dungan **Producer**: Royal Talkies, Newtone Studios **Cinematographer**: Sudhish Ghatak **Story**: Kalidasa **Dialogue**: T. Sadasivam **Lyrics**: Papanasam Sivan **Music**: Rajagopala Sarma **Cast**: M.S. Subbulakshmi, G.N. Balasubramaniam, Serakalathur Sama, N. S. Krishnan, T.S. Dorairaj, T.A. Mathuram, Radha Sadasivam, T.P.S. Mani.

A handsomely mounted adaptation of the Kalidasa epic, *Sakuntalai* is notable for the innovative shooting techniques employed by director Ellis Dungan. These include shooting the pivotal episode of Sakuntala losing her ring in slow motion through a glass water tank. Popular Carnatic singer G.N. Balasubramaniam was cast as the hapless King Dushyant while the legendary M.S. Subbulakshmi played the role of the eponymous nymph, establishing her reputation as a consummate artiste. The film marked the first production by Subbulakshmi and her husband T. S. Sadasivam, who also wrote the screenplay.

Sakuntalai

Khazanchi

Available Material: No original camera negative survives, nor is there a dupe negative.

NFAI: 1 release positive (35 mm), 18 reels, not in a great condition, some of the reels a bit damaged.

17 SUMANGALI

1940, Telugu | B&W, 194 minutes
Director: B. N. Reddy **Producer**: Vauhini Studios **Cinematography, Screenplay**: K. Ramnoth **Dialogue, Lyrics**: Samudrala Raghavacharya **Cast**: Chittor V. Nagaiah, Kumari, M. Lingamurthy, Giri, Malathi, Lingamurthy, Sheshamamba, Doraiswamy.

A reformist melodrama dealing with widow remarriage, *Sumangali* presents the well-worn device of two women in love with the same man. The simple, rustic Parvati (Malathi) is counterposed against the affluent and refined Saraswathi (Kumari), as both fall in love with the progressive Sathyan (Giri). When Saraswathi discovers she had been married and widowed in childhood, the already tangled lives of the three protagonists are thrown into further disarray. The film featured a liberal use of allusive and symbolic imagery, several innovative cinematographic techniques as well as a memorable soundtrack composed by Chittor V. Nagaiah.

Available Material: Film Heritage Foundation tried its best to source any available material of this film from Hyderabad, but

to no avail. The only surviving material is at the NFAI.
NFAI: 1 master positive; 1 release positive, 17 reels; both on 35 mm.

18 KHAZANCHI

1941, Hindi | B&W, 171 minutes
Director: Moti B. Gidwani **Producer**: Pancholi Pictures **Cinematographer**: Badri Dass **Story**: Dalsukh M. Pancholi **Lyrics**: Walli **Music**: Ghulam Haider **Cast**: M.Ismail, Ramola, S.D. Narang, Manorama, Durga Mota, Jankidas, Ajmal.

Besides being the biggest nationwide hit of 1941, *Khazanchi* had a decisive impact on Hindi cinema's editing styles and the presentation of its song sequences. The

soundtrack, with its folk influences, was a trendsetter for Hindi film music, bringing in the Punjabi rhythms which have prevailed ever since. The plot of this Lahore production deals with Shadilal, the titular bank cashier, who is entrusted with the job of transporting gold jewellery to Mumbai. Complications ensue thanks to his son's love affair with a millionaire's daughter and several scandalous developments.

Available Material: The only surviving material of this landmark film from Pancholi Pictures of Lahore is at the NFAI.
NFAI: 1 master positive; 1 combined dupe negative; 1 release positive with a lot of scratches; 14 reels each.

19 SIKANDER

1941, Urdu | B&W, 146 minutes
Director: Sohrab Modi **Producer**: Minerva Movietone **Cinematographer**: Y. D. Sarpotdar **Story, Lyrics**: Sudarshan **Music**: Mir Saheb, Rafiq Ghaznavi **Cast**: Prithviraj Kapoor, Sohrab Modi, Vanamala, Sadiq Ali, K. N. Singh, Meena, Sheela, Zahur Raja, Shakir, Jiloo.

With roots in Parsi theatre and Shakespearean plays, Sohrab Modi was well equipped to make this epic film adaptation of the legendary showdown between the vanquisher Alexander the Great or Sikandar and his potential vassal Porus or Puru, of Punjab. Sikander was played

Kismet

by the dashing Prithviraj Kapoor, while Modi donned the mantle of Porus. The film featured elaborately staged scenes of warfare complete with horses and elephants, alongside grandiose verbal duels enacted with great gusto by acting titans Kapoor and Modi.

Available Material: Originally processed at the Bombay Film Laboratories Pvt. Ltd.
NFAI: 1 master positive; 1 combined dupe negative processed at the FTII lab; 2 release positives with a lot of scratches; all in 16 reels on 35 mm.

20 KISMET

1943, Hindi | B&W, 143 minutes
Director: Gyan Mukherjee **Producer**: Bombay Talkies **Cinematographer**: R.D. Pareenja **Screenplay**: Gyan Mukherjee **Story, Dialogue**: P.L. Santoshi, Shaheed Latif **Lyrics**: Pradeep **Music**: Anil Biswas **Cast**: Ashok Kumar, Mumtaz Shanti, Shahnawaz, Moti, P.F. Pithawala, Chandraprabha, V.H. Desai, Kanu Roy, Jagannath Aurora, Prahlad, Harun, Mubarak, David, Kumari Kamala.

A resounding success when it was first released—the film played for three consecutive years at a theatre in Kolkata—*Kismet* attracted some criticism too, for its morally ambiguous depiction of street crime. The central character Shekhar (Ashok Kumar), a street-wise pickpocket, has no qualms stealing from the rich and the venal in a city riven with inequalities. He is inserted into a convoluted plot involving lost siblings, villainous fathers, stolen necklaces and bumbling policemen. In its exploration of the city and the anti-hero, *Kismet* introduced the striking influence of American film *noir* to the standard expressionist imagery prevalent in the cinema of the times.

Available Material: The only surviving material of this film is with the NFAI. Famous Cine Lab deposited a 15-reel print on 35 mm at the NFAI.
NFAI: 1 master positive; 1 combined dupe negative; 4 release prints of 15 reels each; all on 35 mm. Two of the release positives have a lot of scratches.

Anurag Kashyap on *Kismet*

I have a faint memory of images from *Kismet*: a man in a hat smoking—Ashok

Sikander

Kumar—a street lamp. In fact some of these images are a precursor to my own film *Bombay Velvet*. I feel today we have forgotten to tell stories; we are struggling to tell social stories. To me Noir is in itself a social form of storytelling—practical, adaptable, street philosophy! We have forgotten Noir. It said so much about the changing face of Bombay, a city in transition; about social injustice and social outcasts. The city breeding these characters was fascinating—even today they inhabit my mind. Ashok Kumar in *Kismet* epitomised all this for me.

Salim Khan on *Kismet*

In the list you've made, there is a great film, *Kismet*. The very first film I ever saw as a child! Every one credits Salim-Javed with creating the first anti-hero. But no, the first anti-hero was Ashok Kumar in *Kismet*. People say *Sholay* ran for so many years, but *Kismet* in its time ran successfully for 4 years, in fact longer.

21 UDAYER PATHEY

1944, Bangla | B&W, 121 minutes
Director: Bimal Roy **Producer**: New Theatres **Cinematographer**: Bimal Roy **Story**: Jyotirmoy Roy **Screenplay**: Bimal Roy, Nirmal Dey **Lyrics**: Rabindranath Tagore **Music**: Raichand Boral **Cast**: Radhamohan Bhattacharya, Tulsi Chakroborty, Bishwanath Bhaduri, Rekha Mitra, Binata Basu, Devi Mukherjee, Devbala, Meera Dutta, Boken Chatterjee, Maya Bose, Rajalakshmi, Parul Kar, Manorama, Hiren Basu, Tarapada Choudhury, Smritirekha Biswas, Leena Bose, Aditya Ghosh.

Udeayer Pathey

Bimal Roy's directorial debut was steeped in the staunch socialist ideals that would characterise much of his later work. It spoke of an idealistic, indigent young novelist Anup (Bhattacharya) who serves an exploitative millionaire Rajendranath (Bhaduri). As the millionaire and his son heap indignities upon Anup, his own commitment to the workers' union threatens their business interests. The film marked a remarkable debut for Radhamohan Bhattacharya as the uncompromising *bhadralok* hero, a character reprised in several later films. The title is taken from a Tagore poem.

Available Material: The only surviving material of Bimal Roy's debut film is preserved at the NFAI.
NFAI: 1 dupe negative; 1 sound negative; 3 release positives; 11 reels each, all on 35 mm.

22 MEERA

1945, Tamil | B&W, 136 minutes
Director: Ellis Dungan **Producer**: Chandraprabha Cinetone **Dialogue & Lyrics**: R. Krishnamurthy (Kalki) **Music**: S.V. Venkatraman, Ramnath, Naresh Bhattacharya **Cast**: M.S. Subbulakshmi, M.G. Ramachandran, T.V. Rajasundaribai, S. Santhanam, Kamala Kumari, Chittor V. Nagaiah, T.S. Balaiah.

This adaptation of the legend of Meera—the saint-poetess who devoted her life to Lord Krishna—remains the definitive version since its release in 1945. Apart

Meera

from M.S. Subbulakshmi's performance as Meera, it is her renditions of Meera's *bhajans* that are legendary. The original Tamil film featured some of the best lyric-writing of the eminent Tamil writer Kalki. The film also had a successful Hindi version introduced by poet-politican Sarojini Naidu.

Available Material: The original camera negative does not survive.
NFAI: 1 combined dupe negative, 12 reels; 1 master positive, 13 reels; 3 release prints, 12 reels each; 1 release print, 14 reels; all on 35 mm. 2 release prints, 3 reels each, on 16 mm.

Kamal Haasan on *Meera*

He was 86 when I met this American godfather of Tamil cinema. He created many worthy understudies who become masters of their own domain. The cultural chasm had not deterred him at all: an avid student, he learnt Indian culture along with techniques of cinema. His endeavor must have been as difficult as Mr. Flaherty's, when he made *Nanook of the North*. The film was also made in a Hindi version, for which Mr. Dungan made minute changes in the music to suit the North Indian style. His cognizance astounds me.

23 DHARTI KE LAL

1946, Hindi | B&W, 125 minutes
Director: Khwaja Ahmed Abbas **Producer**: K.A. Abbas, V.P. Sathe, Indian People's Theatre Association (IPTA) **Cinematographer**: Jamnadas Kapadia **Story**: Based on Bijon Bhattacharya's plays *Nabanna* and *Jabanbandi*; Krishan Chander's short

story *Annadata*. **Lyrics**: Ali Sardar Jaffri, Nemichand Jain, Wamiq, Prem Dhawan **Music**: Ravi Shankar **Cast**: Sombhu Mitra, Balraj Sahni, Damayanti Sahni, Anwar Mirza, Usha Dutt, Tripti Bhaduri, Hamid Butt, Pratap Ojha, Rashid Ahmed, Zohra Sehgal, Mahendranath, K.N. Singh, David.

The only film formally produced by the IPTA, it was partly based on Sombhu Mitra's landmark production of the seminal play *Nabanna*, set during the 1943 Bengal famine. The plot deals with the younger son of a peasant family who leaves for the city in search of work when faced with dire circumstances in the village. Thousands of others in a similar predicament make the same journey to the city in his wake. The film was especially notable for introducing a form of stylised realism in its depiction of rural poverty and urban migration, expressly driven by the leftist ideology of its cast and crew. *Dharti ke Lal* prefigured the similarly themed *Do Bigha Zamin*.

Available Material: The original camera negative does not survive.
NFAI: 1 master positive, 13 reels; 2 release positives, 13 reels, lots of scratches

Gosfilmofond, Russia: 1 dupe negative, 13 reels; 1 release positive, 9 reels.

Lekh Tandon on *Dharti ke Lal*

It was the only film produced by the IPTA, admired all over the world. The way it dealt with the famine of Bengal, the realistic presentation was great. It was a first film for many actors, particularly Balraj Sahni.

24 NEECHA NAGAR

1946, Hindi | B&W, 122 minutes
Director: Chetan Anand **Producer**: India Pictures **Cinematography**: Bidyapati Ghosh **Story**: Based on Maxim Gorky's *The Lower Depths* **Screenplay**: Hayatullah Ansari **Lyrics**: Vishwamitter Adil, Manmohan Anand **Music**: Ravi Shankar **Cast**: Rafiq Anwar, Uma Anand, Rafi Peer, Kamini Kaushal, Mohan Sehgal, Zohra Sehgal, Hamid Butt, Prem Kumar.

An adaptation of Gorky's *The Lower Depths* with strong socialist overtones, the film deals with the class divide between a landlord who lives in a house on a hilltop, and the peasants in the valley below, who have to contend with the

Nam Iruvar

refuse flowing down from the landlord's house, spreading sickness and death. The film marked a first outing for sitarist Ravi Shankar as a film composer, and a debut cast that included future acting stalwarts Kamini Kaushal and Zohra Sehgal. It was one of eleven films to be awarded the Grand Prix at the 1st Cannes Film Festival in 1946.

Available Material: The film was considered lost as the original camera negative was burnt in the nitrate fire at Famous, Tardeo. It was a stroke of luck that the great cameraman Subrata Mitra found a print of the film with a scrap dealer in Kolkata and deposited it at the NFAI.
NFAI: 1 dupe negative, 11 reels (with only picture, no sound negative); 2 release prints, 11 reels, both on 35 mm, of which only one is of a quality that can be projected. **Gosfilmofond, Russia:** 1 release positive, 14 reels.

Kamini Kaushal on *Neecha Nagar*
The most unique aspect of the film was the fact that just about every key member of the production team was doing his or her job for the very first time. This film was entirely made by fresh talent. Chetan Anand was directing a film for the first time, and it was a first film for Ravi Shankar and producer Rashid Anwar too. It was very bold of Chetan to work with a fresh cast: Rafique Anwar, Uma Anand, Rafi Peer and Mohan Segal, and of course, I too made my 'casual' debut in that film! None of us had been associated with cinema earlier. Chetan Anand used to be part of the more progressive element of Lahore's literary and creative set. He was the one who got all these first-timers together for *Neecha Nagar*.

Neecha Nagar

WINNER OF THE GRAND PRIZE
INTERNATIONAL FILM FESTIVAL

25 NAM IRUVAR

1947, Tamil | B&W, 153 minutes
Direction: A.V. Meiyappan Chettiar **Producer**: AVM Studios **Cinematography**: T. Muthuswamy **Screenplay**: P. Neelakantan **Lyrics**: Subramanya Bharati **Music**: R. Sudarshanam **Cast**: T.R. Mahalingam, B.R. Panthulu, T.R. Ramachandran, V.K. Ramaswamy, P. Kannamba, K. Sarangapani, T.A. Vijayalakshmi, V.R. Chellam, Kumari Kamala.

The blockbuster film that established the renowned AVM studios, *Nam Iruvar*

was originally a successful stage production. A political melodrama replete with nationalist symbolism and imagery, it tells the story of the two sons of a black-marketeer. The narrative is book-ended by the celebrations of the poet Subramania Bharati's anniversary and the 77th birthday celebrations of Mahatma Gandhi. The musical soundtrack used numerous nationalist songs and love poetry by Bharati, as well as a drum dance that preceded the more famous one in *Chandralekha* (1948).

Available Material: Originally, the film was processed at the AVM Studios lab in Chennai, which is today the only lab that still processes black-and-white film.

AVM Film Studios: 14 reels on 35 mm of picture negative, with no sound negative; 1 release positive, 14 reels, on 35 mm. **NFAI:** 1 release positive, 14 reels, on 35 mm.

---

26 CHANDRALEKHA

1948, Tamil | B&W, 207 minutes
Direction: S.S. Vasan **Producer**: Gemini Studios **Cinematographer**: Kamal Ghosh **Story**: Gemini Story Department **Dialogue**: K.J. Mahadevan, Kothamangalam Subbu, Sangyu, Kittu, Naina **Lyrics**: Papanasam Sivan, Kothamangalam Subbu **Music**: Saluri Rajeshwara Rao **Cast**: T.R. Rajkumari, M.R. Radha, Ranjan, Sundaribai, Surabhi Kamalabai, L. Narayan Rao, P. Subbaiah Pillai, V.N. Janaki, T.A. Mathuram, T.E. Krishnamachariar, N. Seetaraman, Pottai Krishnamurthy.

Mahal

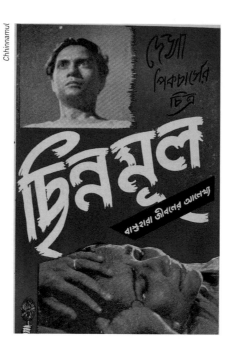

Chhinnamul

Five years in the making, *Chandralekha* was the most ambitious film of its time, the first major bid from a Tamil studio towards all-India distribution. A resounding success across the nation, the film set standards with its lavish production values, and sophisticated marketing and publicity campaign. The swashbuckling period adventure traces the fortunes of the prince Veersimhan (M.R. Radha) and his lover, the fetching Chandralekha (T.R. Rajkumari). When Veerasimhan's father chooses him as the heir to the throne, the younger brother Sasankan (Ranjan) is provoked into unleashing villainy. The film is replete with spectacle and epic sequences, including the longest sword duel in Indian cinema, and a grand climactic drum dance.

Available Material: No original camera negative or dupe negative exists. The only surviving material lies at the NFAI. As a matter of fact, it was S.S. Vasan himself who had a release positive made at his own cost and donated it to the NFAI. It is a tragedy that after his death, no further efforts were made to preserve this historic film. The print at George Eastman House was also received from S. S. Vasan, in 1953.
NFAI: 1 release positive, 20 reels on 35 mm, lots of scratches. **George Eastman House, USA:** 1 35 mm print, 20 reels (18634 feet).

27 ANDAZ

1949, Hindi | B&W, 148 minutes
Direction: Mehboob Khan **Producer:** Mehboob Productions **Cinematography:** Faredoon Irani **Story:** Shams Lucknowi **Screenplay, Dialogue:** Ali Raza **Lyrics:** Majrooh Sultanpuri **Music:** Naushad **Cast:** Dilip Kumar, Nargis, Raj Kapoor, Cuckoo, V.H. Desai, Sapru, Murad, Anwaribai, Amirbano, Jamshedji.

Mehboob Khan's film uses a love story to question the processes of modernisation that were sweeping the newly born nation then. The accent is on cultural and social values with Nargis's Rita, a modern woman who dresses in Western style, caught between a flamboyant lover (Kapoor) and a friend (Kumar) who loves her secretly. The film is known for establishing the screen personas of its stars, besides featuring a sterling soundtrack by Naushad and Majrooh Sultanpuri.

Available Material: Mehboob Khan was a rare filmmaker who cared about preserving his work for posterity. When his studio sent negatives to the Bombay Film Laboratories Pvt. Ltd. to strike prints, he would insist on them being returned to his custody. This is one reason why most of his negatives have survived, and they are preserved to this day in a temporary vault created at Mehboob Studio No. 1.
Mehboob Studios: Original camera negative, 14 reels, processed at the Bombay

Film Laboratories Pvt. Ltd.; 1 release print, 14 reels. **NFAI:** 1 master positive; 1 release positive; 14 reels each.

Nasreen Munni Kabir on *Andaz*
The cinematic language and the treatment of themes in Mehboob's *Andaz* about social class, the complexities of a love triangle and the paranoia of jealousy set the tone for the 1950s' Hindi cinema. Starring Nargis, Dilip Kumar and Raj Kapoor, no other film is as subtle and important in heralding the changing trends.

Jabbar Patel on *Andaz*
Mehboob Khan's black-and-white classic is much ahead of its time. The dilemma of a young girl who has to choose between the two men in her life. It has a strong story, brilliant performances and immortal music. Its unique cinematic treatment still haunts today's filmmakers. It's beyond one's imagination that Mehboob Khan, who joined the film industry as a lightboy, could visualise such a forever-contemporary theme and make this milestone film.

28 MAHAL

1949, Hindi | B&W, 162 minutes
Director: Kamal Amrohi **Producer:** Bombay Talkies **Cinematographer:** Josef Wirsching **Screenplay:** Kamal Amrohi **Lyrics:** Nakshab **Music:** Khemchand Prakash **Cast:** Ashok Kumar, Madhubala, Kumar, Vijayalakshmi, Kanu Roy.

The debut film of director Kamal Amrohi, *Mahal* is considered a classic of Hindi cinema. A ghost story which shades into dark psychological drama, the film also incorporates elements of reincarnation to create a new Indian Gothic genre. The complicated plot deals with Shankar (Kumar) who comes to a haunted mansion, and discovers a connection with its tragic past. He encounters a mysterious spirit in the house and gradually becomes obsessed with her, driving himself to the brink of insanity. The film featured some of the best work done by cameraman Josef Wirsching, as well as a haunting soundtrack by Khemchand Prakash which features the Lata Mangeshkar track 'Aayega aayega'.

Available Material: There is an interesting story to the preservation of this film. Bombay Talkies went into liquidation and as a result the print of *Mahal* landed up in the custody of A.N. Khare, the Official Liquidator at the time. Abdul Ali of the Cine Society managed to get a print of *Mahal* out of his custody. Kapurchand Brothers, distributors and owners of Roxy Cinema acquired the rights to the film and re-released it at Roxy Cinema in Mumbai in 1975, where it ran for ten to twelve weeks in the matinee slot. Post its run at the cinema, the print was deposited at the NFAI.

NFAI: 1 master positive; 1 release positive; 16 reels each.

29 CHHINNAMUL

1950, Bengali | B&W, 117 minutes
Director: Nemai Ghosh **Producer**: Desha Pictures **Cinematographer**: Nemai Ghosh **Screenplay, Lyrics**: Swarnkamal Bhattacharya **Music**: Kalabaran Das **Cast**: Prematosh Roy, Gangapada Basu, Shobha Sen, Shanta Devi, Shanti Mitra, Sushil Sen, Jalad Chatterjee, Bijon Bhattacharya, Ritwik Ghatak.

Chhinnamul is notable for being the first direct cinematic exploration of the horrors of the partition of the subcontinent. Its immediacy was evidenced by its use of mostly untrained actors playing themselves, and often playing out their own ordeals on the screen. More a collage of stories of partition refugees than a coherent narrative, the film featured several scenes of a very high emotional register. Surviving court directives and police harassment, the film was released with the intervention of B. N. Sircar of New Theatres. A commercial failure, the film saw a revival of fortunes when it was bought and released in the USSR at the recommendation of the Russian master Vsevolod Pudovkin.

Available Material: No original camera negative survives. The only surviving material available is at the NFAI.
NFAI: 1 master positive; 3 release positives; all on 35 mm, 11 reels. **Gosfilmofond, Russia:** 1 release positive in Bengali, 11 reels; 1 release positive in Russian, 9 reels.

Girish Kasaravalli on *Chhinnamul*
　Chhinnamul appeared before *Pather Panchali*, the first major film from India. It had all the traits of a neo-realist film, which deeply influenced my work. As a student of cinema, I feel that restoring this film would help lovers of Indian cinema understand our film heritage from a different perspective.

30 AWAARA

1951, Hindi | B&W, 193 minutes
Director: Raj Kapoor **Producer**: R.K. Films **Cinematographer**: Radhu Karmakar **Story**: K.A. Abbas, V.P. Sathe **Screenplay, Dialogue**: K.A. Abbas **Lyrics**: Hasrat Jaipuri, Shailendra **Music**: Shankar-Jaikishen **Cast**: Raj Kapoor, Nargis, Prithviraj Kapoor, Leela Chitnis, K.N. Singh

Raj Kapoor's famous film, a smash hit across India which brought its lead stars fame in the USSR and the Arab world as well. A melodrama dealing with class divides, the film brims over with intriguing Oedipal overtones—Prithviraj Kapoor and Raj Kapoor, father and son in real life, portray the same relationship on screen. The film abounds with musical numbers, including the spectacularly mounted *'Ghar aaya mera pardesi'*, which builds a hallucinatory dreamscape to depict the intense inner turmoil of the lead character. The film remains a popular favourite to this day and is considered a classic of the Hindi commercial cinema.

Andaz

112

Available Material: The original camera negative does not exist. Originally processed at Famous Cine Laboratory, Tardeo, the film's material is with R.K. Films, stored in their vault at R.K. Studios. The NFAI's master positive was made from the dupe negative given by Raj Kapoor. Several 16 mm prints are also available with private collectors.
R. K. Films: 1 dupe negative; 1 release positive; both 19 reels. **NFAI**: 1 master positive, 19 reels; 3 release positives, 19 reels each, quite scratched. **TIFF Bell Lightbox, Canada**: 1 print, 19 reels. **Gosfilmofond, Russia**: 1 release positive, 19 reels; 1 release positive of 2 parts, 8 reels each.

Amitabh Bachchan on *Awaara*

This film is etched in my mind. Made at a time when India was newly independent, the approach of the film was socialist. K.A. Abbas *saheb* and Raj-*ji* constructed the story according to the times. Talking about Raj-*ji*'s incredible showmanship—in our country where cinema is seen as entertainment, the story angle was so unique. He envisioned the dream sequence in the film in a way never seen before. You are amazed by his fantastical imagination. The surreal setting, ethereal Nargis-*ji* emerging through thick clouds of smoke, Raj-*ji* surrounded by demonic figures and burning fires: there is such a powerful, mystical symbolism in the dream sequence.

Do Bigha Zamin

31 MALLEESHWARI

1951, Telugu | B&W, 194 minutes
Director: B.N. Reddy **Producer**: Vauhini Studios
Cinematographer: Adi M. Irani, B.N. Konda
Reddy **Story**: Based on Buchi Babu's play *Rayalvari Karunkritiyamu* **Screenplay, Lyrics**: Devalupalli Krishna Sastry **Music**: Saluri Rajeswara Rao **Cast**: P. Bhanumathi, N.T. Rama Rao, Kumari, T.G. Kamladevi, Srivastava, Rushyendramani, Baby Mallika, Doraiswamy, Venkatramana.

B. N. Reddy's opulently mounted musical is set in the court of Krishnadev Raya, king of the Vijayanagara Empire. It is the story of Malleeshwari (Bhanumathi) and a sculptor named Nagaraja (Rao) who love each other, but are kept apart by class differences. Further complications arise when Malleeshwari's beauty draws the king's attention, and she is summoned

to the court to become a dancer. The film featured magnificent sets created by A.K. Sekhar, as well as a very popular soundtrack.

Available Material: No material of this film survives anywhere except for what has been preserved at the NFAI.
NFAI: 1 master positive; 1 dupe negative; 1 release positive; each 19 reels.

Malleeshwari

K. Viswanath on *Malleeshwari*

Malleeshwari is very special to me. I was a sound recordist at Vauhini Studios, Madras (now Chennai) and actually worked for this film. It reminds me of the early days of my career and the respect and admiration I continue to have for the many contributors to this classic: director B.N. Reddy *garu*, art director Sri A.K. Sekhar *garu*, cinematographer Sri Adi Irani *garu*, music director Sri S Rajeshwar Rao *garu*, lyricist Sri Devupalli Krishna Sastri *garu*, the actors Sri N.T. Rama Rao *garu* and Smt. P Bhanumati *garu*. I know how much labour and devotion has gone into shaping the film's exemplary music, meaningful songs, lyrical photography, spell-binding performances, and technical finesse—all under the exacting stewardship of Sri B.N.Reddy *garu*. *Malleeshwari*'s charm and pull is timeless. Such timelessness must be preserved. In my opinion, it will stimulate and continue to inspire both aspiring and practicing members in all departments of film-making.

32 PARASAKTHI

1952, Tamil | B&W, 188 minutes
Director: R. Krishnan, S. Panju **Producer**: AVM Productions, National Pictures **Story**: M.S. Balasundaram **Screenplay, Dialogue**: M. Karunanidhi **Lyrics**: M. Karunanidhi, Bharatidasan, Subramanya Bharati, K.N. Anualthango, K.P. Kamakshisundaram, Udumalai Narayana Kavi **Music**: R. Sudarshanam **Cast**: Sivaji Ganesan, S.S. Rajendran, S.V. Sahasranamam, Sriranjani Jr., Pandharibai, Kannamma, V.K. Ramaswamy, Kumari Kamala

Parasakthi follows the lives of three brothers and a sister during the World War II period. Amidst nationalist struggles, wartime hardships, and the vagaries of fate, what come through most explicitly in the film is a castigation of the brahmanical order and an unyielding commitment to reason and social justice. This seminal film is almost a cinematic testament to the ideals of the Dravidian movement in Tamil Nadu, scripted by one of its stalwarts: future chief minister and DMK supremo M. Karunanidhi. It is remembered also for Sivaji Ganesan's breakthrough performance, especially his impassioned climactic monologue in a packed courtroom.

Available Material: The film was originally processed at the AVM Film Studios lab. **AVM Film Studios:** 1 married dupe nega-

Devadasu

tive,17 reels, not in a great condition; 1 release positive, 17 reels.
NFAI: 1 master positive; 2 release positives; 17 reels each.

Adoor Gopalakrishnan on *Parasakthi*

Parasakthi is one film that marked the departure from the spectacular and mythological films which were in vogue in Tamil. Although it did make compromises based on commercial demands, the treatment of the subject was realistic to a great extent, and the film questioned many of the wrongs that reigned over society at large. In this film we had M. Karunanidhi, the fiery writer of the left, penning the script and the great actor Sivaji Ganeshan making his debut performance on screen.

---

33 DEVADASU

1953, Telugu | B&W, 188 minutes
Director: Vedantam Ragavaiah **Producer**: Vinoda Pictures **Cinematographer**: B.S. Ranga **Story**: Based on Saratchandra Chattopadhyay's novel *Devdas* **Dialogue**: Samudrala Raghavacharya **Lyrics**: Samudrala Raghavacharya **Music**: C.R. Subburaman **Cast**: A. Nageswara Rao, Savitri, Lalitha, C.S.R. Anjaneyulu, Doraiswamy, S.V. Ranga Rao.

The first Telugu adaptation of the tale of Devdas, the archetypal lovelorn alcoholic, it featured Telugu acting giant Akkineni Nageswara Rao in the eponymous role. Savitri starred as Paro, Devdas's childhood friend and lover, cruelly separated from him by circumstances

Parasakthi

and social hierarchy, while Lalitha played the role of the golden-hearted prostitute Chandramukhi. The film featured a hugely popular soundtrack by the eminent music composer C.R. Subburaman.

Available Material: No original camera negative survives. The only surviving material is at the NFAI.
NFAI: 1 release positive (35 mm), 19 reels.

Adoor Gopalakrishnan on *Devadasu*

I saw *Devadasu* while I was in school and I was deeply impressed by the performances of Nageswara Rao and Savitri. The film was very faithful to Saratchandra's story. Although there have been many different versions, *Devadasu* stands apart in its powerful portrayal of the roles of Devadas and his love.

---

34 DO BIGHA ZAMIN

1953, Hindi | B&W, 142 minutes
Director: Bimal Roy **Producer**: Bimal Roy Productions **Cinematographer**: Kamal Bose **Story**: Salil Chaudhury **Screenplay**: Hrishikesh Mukherjee **Dialogue**: Paul Mahendra **Lyrics**: Shailendra **Music**: Salil Chaudhury **Cast**: Balraj Sahni, Nirupa Roy, Murad, Rattan Kumar, Nana Palshikar, Meena Kumari, Jagdeep, Nasir Hussain, Mehmood, Mishra, Dilip Jr., Nandkishore, Rajlakshmi, Noor, Kusum, Hiralal, Sapru, Tiwari.

Profoundly inspired by the Italian neo-realist cinema, Bimal Roy relinquished studio sets for shooting on actual locations in the countryside and on city

Jhansi ki Rani

future filmmaker. It was one of the earliest attempts at neo-realism, combining it with a dramatic narrative structure to create a work which had both an aesthetic appeal and popular appreciation.

Nirad N. Mohapatra on *Do Bigha Zamin*

Do Bigha Zamin is a daring experiment within the parameters of mainstream cinema. Influenced by neo-realism, the film took its camera to the streets of Kolkata and spoke of many social issues, including migration of rural farm labour to the metros in search of greener pastures. It certainly was a path-breaking film that needs to be preserved for posterity.

35 JHANSI KI RANI

1953, Hindi | Colour, 148 minutes
Director: Sohrab Modi **Producer**: Minerva Movietone **Cinematographer**: Ernest Haller **Story**: S.R. Dubey **Screenplay**: Geza Herczeg, Sudarshan, Adi F. Keeka **Dialogue**: Munshi Abdul Baqui, Shams Lucknowi **Lyrics**: Radheshyam Kathavachak **Music**: Vasant Desai **Cast**: Mehtab, Sohrab Modi, Mubarak, Ulhas, Sapru, Ramsingh, Anil Kishore, Baby Shikha.

Another one of Sohrab Modi's magnificently mounted historical epics, this film is based on the life of the valiant Rani Laxmibai of Jhansi who fought to protect the sovereignty of her kingdom against the marauding East India Company. The film was shot in spectacular, vivid colour by the great Hollywood cinematographer Ernest Haller (*Gone with the Wind, Rebel Without a Cause, Mildred Pierce*) and featured enormous battle scenes (courtesy the Ministry of Defence) with ranks of soldiers and animals from the royal kingdoms of Bikaner and Jaipur.

Available Material: The film was shot using 35 mm Three-Strip Technicolor process. The cinematographer Ernest Haller was selected for his artistry and experience in shooting with the Three-Strip Technicolor film and camera. As there were no facilities at that time for colour processing in India, all the processing was done at the Technicolor Laboratories in the UK. (The total length of film exposed for Technicolor was approximately 250,000 feet and the total soundtrack used was about 200,000 feet.) The orig-

streets. The tale of Shambu Mahato (Balraj Sahni) and his family caught in a downward spiral of debt and poverty was narrated with such searing honesty and fierce humanism, that it has branded itself in the consciousness of cinephiles ever since. Winner of both the 1st National Award for Best Feature Film in India and the International Prize at the 7th Cannes Film Festival, the film remains a benchmark for viewers, filmmakers, film scholars and historians alike.

Available Material: In March 2009, the Bombay Film Laboratories Pvt. Ltd. handed over 13 reels of the original camera negative and 13 reels of the sound negative to the Bimal Roy family, which were later deposited by them at the NFAI. Unfortunately by this time the original camera negative had already decomposed. **NFAI:** 1 master positive; 1 dupe negative (picture only); 1 sound negative; 1 release positive of 13 reels; each on 35 mm. The release positive has mould problems. **BFI:** 1 dupe negative on 35 mm; 1 dupe negative on 16 mm; both 13 reels. **The National Film Archive of the Czech Republic:** 1 nitrate dupe negative; 1 release positive, 13 reels; both on 35 mm.

Saeed Akhtar Mirza on *Do Bigha Zamin*

The deep humanism of *Do Bigha Zamin* left a very lasting impression on me as a inal three-strip negative of the film and its soundtrack was then archived and stored at the Technicolor Laboratories in London until 1990. In 1990, the BFI (British Film Institute) National Archive acquired the materials from Technicolor and stored them in the BFI's main archive location at Berkhamsted in the UK, which is where they remain to this day. The film was earlier processed in 17 reels, but is now preserved in 9 reels each of yellow, cyan and magenta strips at the BFI. The combined dupe negative at the NFAI was deposited by the Bombay Film Laboratories Pvt. Ltd.

BFI: Original three-strip negative, 9 reels; original sound negative, 9 reels. **NFAI**: 1 master positive; 1 release positive; 1 combined dupe negative; 17 reels each.

36 SHYAMCHI AAI

1953, Marathi | B&W, 152 minutes
Director: Prahlad Keshav Atre **Producer**: Atre Pictures **Cinematographer**: R.M. Rele **Story**: Based on Sane Guruji's novel *Shyamchi Aai* **Screenplay**: P.K. Atre **Lyrics**: P.K. Atre, Vasant Bapat, Rajkavi Yeshwant **Music**: Vasant Desai **Cast**: Vanamala, Madhu Vaze, Umesh, Baburao Pendharkar, Damuanna Joshi, Sumati Gupte, Saraswati Bodas, Vasant Bapat, Prabodhankar Thakre, Nagesh Joshi, Bapurao Mane, Pandurang Joshi, Vimal Ghaisas.

Based on Sanu Guruji's eponymous auto-biographical book, one of the most important works in modern Marathi literature, *Shyamchi Aai* was adapted and directed by P.K. Atre, another renowned Marathi writer. Essentially a series of memories narrated in flashback, the film depicts the author's poverty-stricken childhood in the Konkan region of Maharashtra, growing up with the teachings of his mother, whom he idolised. Vanmala played the devout venerable mother, who has an earthy, practical philosophy of her own. The film has remained a landmark in Marathi cinema ever since its release. It won the President's Medal for Best Feature Film at the first National Film Awards ceremony in 1954.

Available Material: No original camera negative exists. Given the film's great popularity at the time and the fact that it was regularly shown across Maharashtra in tent cinemas, several 16 mm prints of the film are still in existence. NFDC has deposited a dupe negative at the NFAI.

NFAI: 1 master positive, 15 reels; 1 dupe negative, 15 reels (NFDC); 3 release positives, 15 reels; 1 sound negative, 9 reels.

Gulzar on *Shyamchi Aai*

Shyamchi Aai is important because the film marks the beginning of our National Awards. The film won the Best Film award, which then was called the President's Award.

37 ANDHA NAAL

1954, Tamil | B&W, 130 minutes
Director: Sundaram Balachander **Producer**: AVM Studios **Cinematographer**: Maruthi Rao **Screenplay, Dialogue**: Javar Seetharaman **Cast**: Sivaji Ganesan, Pandari Bai, Javar Seetaraman, P.D. Sambandam, T.K. Balachandran, Menaka, Suryakala.

Andha Naal was the first emphatic example of experimentation in Tamil cinema. Said to be loosely based on Akira Kurosawa's *Rashomon*, the film was a stark police procedural about the murder of a radio operator, entirely bereft of song and dance. Packed with plot twists, the narrative was presented through the perspectives of different characters. AVM Studios, after the stupendous success of the epic *Parasakthi*, was initially loath to produce a songless film which featured

their newly minted star Sivaji Ganesan as an unsavoury character. Over the years, the film has become a stylistic reference point, often cited as the earliest example of film *noir* in Tamil cinema.

Available Material: No original camera negative survives.
AVM Film Studios: 1 combined dupe negative, 15 reels, on 35 mm. **NFAI**: 1 release positive, 15 reels.

Mani Ratnam on *Andha Naal*

Andha Naal is a landmark film in Tamil Cinema in more than one sense. It was the first film without a song-and-dance sequence. A film in which a leading star of the era played an outright negative role. *Andha Naal* was a radical breakaway from the norm in its time and continues to remain so. It is a very significant film in Tamil film history, easily one of the best ever made. To me, the film was a revelation: in my journey of understanding cinema, it was a major stepping stone. I strongly feel that this masterpiece should be restored.

38 BEDARA KANNAPPA

1954, Kannada | B&W, 152 minutes
Director: H.L.N. Simha **Producer**: Gubbi Karnataka Films **Screenplay**: G.V. Iyer **Music**: R. Sudarshanam **Cast**: Rajkumar, Pandharibai, G.V. Iyer, Narsimharaju.

Andha Naal

Bedara Kannappa

The film marked the debut of Kannada matinee idol Rajkumar. A quasi-mythological melodrama in the 'folklore' genre, it was an adaptation by G.V. Iyer of his own play, marking his screenwriting debut. Dinna (Rajkumar) and Neela (Pandharibai) are gods banished to earth, where they are born to a tribe of hunters. The narrative, which followed their trials and tribulations in the human world, served as the archetype for later films, establishing a typically Kannada genre in which human beings often turn out to be gods among us.

Available Material: No original camera negative or dupe negative of this film survives. The present copyright holder, Shree Ganesh Video in Bangalore, has a master positive in good condition.
Shree Ganesh Video: 1 master positive, 16 reels (4270.55 metres). **NFAI:** 1 release positive, 16 reels on 35 mm, very poor condition.

39 NEELAKUYIL

1954, Malayalam | B&W, 182 minutes
Director: P. Bhaskaran, Ramu Kariat **Producer:** Chandrathara Pictures **Cinematography:** A. Vincent **Story:** Uroob (P.C. Kuttikrishnan) **Lyrics:** P. Bhaskaran **Music:** K. Raghavan **Cast:** Kumari, P. Bhaskaran, Prema, Sathyan, Kodangallur Ammini Amma, Master Vipin, Manavalan Joseph, Balakrishna Menon, Kochappan, Balaraman, J.A.R. Anand, Johnson, V. Abdullah, V. Kamakshi, Thangamani.

A major breakthrough in its time, *Neelakuyil* inaugurated a trend of realist melodrama which continued in Malayalam cinema over the next 20 years. Ramu Kariat's debut film introduced a new idiom, employing the naturalist performance styles of new actors like Sathyan to portray themes from the reformist literature of novelist Uroob. The narrative deals with a high-caste village postman who adopts the illegitimate child of a Harijan girl, creating a furore in his deeply conservative village which ultimately compels the actual father to acknowledge his paternity. The film was also a musical hit, remembered for its songs.

Available Material: No original camera negative survives.
NFAI: 1 master positive; 2 release positives; each 19 reels, on 35 mm.

40 DEVDAS

1955, Hindi | B&W, 159 minutes
Director: Bimal Roy **Producer:** Bimal Roy Productions **Cinematographer:** Kamal Bose **Story:** Based on Saratchandra Chattopadhyay's novel *Devdas* **Screenplay:** Nabendu Ghosh **Dialogue:** Rajinder Singh Bedi **Lyrics:** Sahir Ludhianvi **Music:** S.D. Burman **Cast:** Dilip Kumar, Suchitra Sen, Vyjayanthimala, Motilal, Kanhaiyalal, Nasir Hussain.

An updated version of Barua's 1936 film on which director Bimal Roy had served as cinematographer, *Devdas* features Dilip Kumar as the intensely brooding hero, Suchitra Sen as his tragic unattainable love, and Vyjayanthimala as the graceful dancer whose ebullience conceals deep emotion. The melodramatic tale was well served by Kamal Bose's expert cinematography and the soundtrack by S.D. Burman and Sahir Ludhianvi. True to Roy's concerns, the film manages to look beyond Devdas's obsessions at society as a whole, depicting a decadent, feudal world which mercilessly crushes any quest for personal happiness and redemption.

Available Material: No original camera negative survives. 10 reels of the original camera negative were handed over in March 2009 by Bombay Film Laboratories Pvt. Ltd. to the Bimal Roy family, but these reels did not survive as they had decomposed. The dupe negative in possession of the NFAI was given to them by Bombay Film Laboratories Pvt. Ltd. along with the original camera negative of Bimal Roy's *Benazir* (1964).
NFAI: 1 dupe negative, 18 reels; 3 release positives, 18 reels; all on 35 mm.

Amitabh Bachchan on *Devdas*

Another one of my favourite films is Bimal Roy's *Devdas*. I still remember Dilip *saheb*'s performance: for my generation, his Devdas will always be the ultimate performance. Bimal Roy-*ji*'s knowledge of Bengali literature and its nuances, his understanding of Saratbabu's writing, the star cast, the outstanding performances, and the music came together to create an iconic film that will remain with us eternally.

41 MISSIAMMA

1955, Tamil | B&W, 179
Director: L.V. Prasad **Producer:** Vijaya Pictures
Co-Producers: B. Nagi Reddy, Chakrapani
Cinematography: Marcus Bartley **Screenplay:** Chakrapani **Dialogue, Lyrics:** Thanjai Ramaiyadas **Music:** Saluri Rajeshwara Rao **Cast:** Savitri, Jamuna, S.V. Ranga Rao, Rushyendramani, Gemini Ganesan, K.A. Thangavelu, Relangi Venkataramaiah, Balakrishna, Ramanna Reddy, Gummadi Venkateswara Rao, M.N. Nambiar, A. Karunanidhi, V.M. Ezhumalai, Santhanam, Meenakshi.

A comedy involving mistaken identities, the film tells the story of unemployed Rao (Ganesan) and Mary (Savitri), who have to pretend to be married to each other in order to find jobs as teachers in a village school. This entertaining hit film was an adaptation of a classic Bengali comedy, and was in turn remade in Hindi and Marathi. It established the lead screen pair of Gemini Ganesan and Savitri and featured a hit soundtrack with track *'Varaye vennilave'* becoming especially popular.

Available Material: No original camera negative survives. Vijaya Pictures, Vijaywada, the present negative copyright holder, has a dupe negative of 18 reels (they have edited out one reel). One release positive of the Telugu version survives with Goldstone Technologies in Hyderabad.

Vijaya Pictures: 1 dupe negative, 18 reels. **Goldstone Technologies:** 1 release positive, 19 reels. **NFAI:** 1 master positive; 1 release positive of the Tamil version; both 19 reels; both not in good condition. The master positive has vinegar syndrome and has shrunk

42 SHRI 420

1955, Hindi | B&W, 177 minutes
Director: Raj Kapoor **Producer**: R.K. Films
Cinematographer: Radhu Karmakar **Story**: K.A. Abbas **Screenplay**: K.A. Abbas, V.P. Sathe **Lyrics**: Shailendra, Hasrat Jaipuri **Music**: Shankar-Jaikishen **Cast**: Raj Kapoor, Nargis, Nadira, Lalita Pawar, Nana Palshikar, Pesi Patel, Nemo, M. Kumar, Hari Shivdasani, Bhudo Advani, Iftikhar, Sheila Vaz, Ramesh Sinha, Rashid Khan.

A relatively straightforward morality tale contrasting the essentially decent poor classes and the corrupt rich, this is the film which confirmed Raj Kapoor's persona of the naïve, endearing tramp. Here, the character of the vagabond is sucked into a vortex of greed and crime, seduced by the temptress Maya (Nadira) who draws him into a decadent life, and ultimately rescued by the love of the poor schoolteacher Vidya (Nargis). The soundtrack featured songs that have become iconic in Hindi cinema, such as the rain-drenched duet *'Pyaar hua ikraar hua'*, and the declaration of Indianness in *'Mera joota hai japani'*.

Available Material: Originally processed at the Famous Cine Laboratory, Tardeo, the original camera negative does not survive. Several 16 mm prints are available with private collectors.
R.K. Films: 1 dupe negative, 19 reels; 1 release positive, 19 reels. **NFAI:** 3 release positives, 19 reels each.

Rajkumar Hirani on *Shri 420*
We grew up on songs like *'Pyar Hua Ikrar Hua'*, *'Ramaiyya Vasta Vaiyya'* and *'Dil Ka Haal Sune Dilwala'*... I would love to see the Raj Kapoor-Nargis classic *Shri 420* restored and back on screen.

43 JAGTE RAHO

1956, Hindi | B&W, 149 minutes
Director: Sombhu Mitra, Amit Maitra **Producer**: R.K. Films **Cinematographer**: Radhu Karmakar **Screenplay**: Sombhu Mitra, Amita Maitra **Dialogue**: K.A. Abbas **Lyrics**: Shailendra, Prem Dhawan **Cast**: Raj Kapoor, Pradeep Kumar, Smriti Biswas, Motilal, Moni Chatterjee, Bikram Kapoor, Bhupendra Kapoor, Bhudo Advani, Krishnakant, Pran, Ratan, Gaurang, Rashid Khan, Nargis.

A comical, critical depiction of middle-class life, *Jagte Raho* shows the travails of a thirsty peasant (Kapoor) who strays into an apartment building in search of water, launching a series of misadventures. The comedy acquires a darker dimension as the night stretches on, and

Neelakuyil

Shri 420

Pyaasa

ultimately delivers a searing denuncia-
tion of bourgeois apathy and the erosion
of humanist values in India. The film was
an unusual collaboration for Raj Kapoor's
studio with the Bengali PTA director
Sombhu Mitra. The film became successful only after a shortened version won the
main prize at the Karlovy Vary festival in
1957. As the years have gone by, it only
seems increasingly prophetic.

Available Material: In a rare occurrence,
R.K. Films has the original camera negative of this film on 35 mm, as well as the
sound negative. They have also preserved
the Bengali version of the film.
R. K. Films: Original camera negative, 14
reels, on 35 mm; 1 sound negative, 14
reels.

NFAI: 1 master positive; 1 release positive; both 14 reels. **Gosfilmofond, Russia:**
1 release positive, 14 reels; 1 release positive in Russian in two parts of 7 reels
each.

Jahnu Barua on *Jagte Raho*
I consider Amit Maitra's *Jagte Raho* to be
a great cinematic statement on humanity getting lost with the advent of material
living. As the world starts growing more
and more inclined towards urban life, society tends to get delinked from basic human
values. *Jagte Raho* beautifully presents
a metaphoric criticism on each human
aspect, through a series of events experienced by the protagonist one night in an
apartment building which he has entered in
search of some water to quench his thirst.

Jagte Raho is undoubtedly an important
Indian classic that must be preserved for its
content and cinematic treatment.

44 PYAASA

1957, Hindi | B&W, 153 minutes
Director: Guru Dutt **Producer**: Guru Dutt Films
Cinematographer: V.K. Murthy **Dialogue**: Abrar Alvi
Lyrics: Sahir Ludhianvi **Music**: S.D. Burman **Cast**:
Guru Dutt, Waheeda Rehman, Mala Sinha, Johnny
Walker, Rehman, Kumkum, Shyam, Leela Mishra,
Rajinder, Mayadass, Mehmood, Radheshyam,
Ashita, Moni Chatterjee

A classic melodrama about a misunder-
stood romantic artist, *Pyaasa* was a landmark film for actor-director Guru Dutt,
and a great popular success. Its principal
character is the unsuccessful poet Vijay,
who rejects his family to live on the
streets, where he encounters the prostitute Gulabo. The narrative traces his har-
rowing journey to hold on to his artistic
integrity and lay claim to his own work
in a corrupt and materialistic world.
Cinematographer V.K. Murthy creates
striking evocative images; the memorable
soundtrack, lauded by *Sight and Sound* as
'one of the best ever in film', ranges from
the bitter rhetoric of '*Jinhen naaz hai*' to
the bemused resignation of '*Jaane woh
kaise*' to the ultimate aria of world-weary
disillusionment, '*Yeh duniya agar mil
bhi jaye to kya hai.*'

Available Material: Originally processed at
the Famous Cine Lab, Tardeo, one of the
oldest labs in Mumbai, the original camera negative does not survive.
NFAI: 1 dupe negative, 16 reels; 3 release
positives, 16 reels each.

Shekhar Kapur on *Pyaasa*
Pyaasa is a film I watch again and again.
It never fails to move me for its ability to
convey its message in a very simple way.
Yes, it may at times be simplistic. But the
use of light and shade, and the amazing use
of music to convey emotions, makes this
film stand out as a masterpiece of Indian
cinema. Sadly, colour brought a garishness
to Indian commercial cinema that we are
yet to get over. It means dazzle now. But
in Guru Dutt's B&W films, the use of light
and shadows brought a sophistication of

story-telling that is still hard to find.

Naseeruddin Shah on *Pyaasa*

Pyaasa is one of the most significant films made in our country and that it is languishing in need of restoration is indicative of the apathy that is our besetting sin.

Suresh Chhabria on *Pyaasa*

Guru Dutt's *Pyaasa* is a report card on the tenth anniversary of Indian independence from a romantic poet. Every sequence is suffused with pain and longing threaded together with themes of disillusionment and the allure of renunciation. Perhaps never again did Indian popular cinema achieve the same balance between personal vision, melodrama and social criticism. Dutt's artistic conviction transfigures the stereotypes, clichés and coincidences and elevates them to the stuff of supreme poetic expression. The song sequences and the lyrics by Sahir Ludhianvi are by themselves an anthology of the best elements of Bombay cinema's synthesis of socio-religious imagery and formal eclecticism.

45 MAYA BAZAAR

1957, Telugu | B&W, 192 minutes
Director: K.V. Reddy **Producer**: Vijaya Pictures
Cinematographer: Marcus Bartley
Screenplay: Chakrapani **Lyrics**: Pingali Nagendra Rao **Music**: Ghantasala Venkateshwara Rao
Cast: N.T. Rama Rao, S.V. Ranga Rao, Akkineni Nageswara Rao C.S.R. Anjaneyulu, Savitri, Relangi Venkatramaiah, Gummadi Venkateshwara Rao, K. Mukkamala, Rajanala Nageshwara Rao, Savitri, Vangara, Balakrsihna, Rushyendramani, Suryakantam, Chhaya Devi, Sandhya.

A mythological from the Vijaya studios, the film adapts an episode from the *Mahabharata* which has been elaborated with stunts, special effects, comedy and musical numbers in countless stage and screen adaptations. The plot deals with the marriage of Abimanyu (Nageswara Rao) to Sasirekha (Savitri), aided by the rakshas Ghatothkach (Ranga Rao), son of the Pandava hero Bhima. The film featured actor and future politician N.T. Rama Rao in his first appearance as the god Krishna.

Available Material: Goldstone Technologies in Hyderabad has the original cam-

Maya Bazaar

era negative of the Telugu version in only seven double reels. The original film had ten double reels. The only reason the film has survived is because it was so popular that even years after its release, it was being screened at some theatre or the other, and new prints were always being struck. In 2007, the company bought all the existing prints they could find, taking them out of circulation since they planned to release a colourised version. Vijaya Pictures, Vijaywada, the present negative copyright holder, has a dupe negative of 19 reels of the Telugu version (they have edited out one reel).
Goldstone Technologies: Original camera negative, 7 double reels. **Vijaya Pictures:** Dupe negative, 19 reels. **NFAI:** 1 master positive; 1 release positive; 20 reels each, only the Tamil version.

46 MOTHER INDIA

1957, Hindi | Colour, 168 minutes
Director: Mehboob Khan **Producer**: Mehboob Productions **Cinematographer**: Faredoon Irani
Screenplay: Mehboob Khan **Dialogue**: Wajahat Mirza, S. Ali Raza **Lyrics**: Shakeel Badayuni **Music**: Naushad **Cast**: Nargis, Sunil Dutt, Rajendra Kumar, Raaj Kumar, Kanhaiyalal, Jiloo, Kumkum, Master Sajid, Sitara Devi.

Rich in incident and spectacle, director Mehboob Khan's *Mother India* has acquired the status of a national epic over the years. A remake of Khan's own *Aurat* (1940), the film unfolds the saga of a peasant woman (Nargis in an iconic performance), whose courage and determination symbolises the endurance of the nation itself. The rural landscapes of India, the rhythms of village life and the changing seasons are brought alive by evocative colour cinematography in rich earth tones. Showered with awards after its release (including two National Awards), *Mother India* was also the first Indian film to make it to the final list of nominees for the Best Foreign Language Film at the Academy Awards.

Available Material: Originally shot on Gevacolor (Belgium), the film was processed at Film Centre, Mumbai. The original camera negative was then sent to the Technicolor Lab in London for taking out prints and the original camera negative was preserved at the lab till it was shifted to the Pinewood Film Lab. When this lab shut down, the original camera negative was sent back to India and is now with Mehboob Studios.
Mehboob Studios: Original camera negative, 19 reels (15642 feet) **NFAI:** 1 release positive, 10 double reels. **Gosfilmofond, Russia:** 1 release positive in Russian in two parts – the first part in 8 reels and the second in 9 reels.

Amitabh Bachchan on *Mother India*

Today, in our country we have been talking about women empowerment, but if you look at Nargis-*ji*'s performance in *Mother India*, a film made in 1957, she was

Do Aankhen Barah Haath

the epitome of the empowered woman—
the strength of a woman, the strength of a
mother so powerfully portrayed against the
landscape of rural India. The way Mehboob
saheb captured the lives of the people living
in the villages of India and the performances
of Dutt *saheb* and Raaj Kumar *saheb* still
remains embedded in our mind. And how
can I forget the wonderful performance of
Kanhaiyalal-*ji*. What a star cast! Being from
U.P. myself, the film really resonated with
me. It is like a canvas well-painted.

Saeed Akhtar Mirza on *Mother India*

It's the epic story of a nation being born,
from the colonial past to a modern republic.
Perhaps the inspiration was D.W. Griffith's
The Birth of a Nation, but Mehboob Khan
went beyond it to tell the tale of an ordinary
rural woman who struggles with the loss of
her land and also to bring up her two sons
to be honourable citizens of an emerging
free India.

47 DO AANKHEN BARAH HAATH

1957, Hindi | B&W, 155 minutes
Director: V. Shantaram **Producer**: Rajkamal
Kalamandir **Cinematographer**: G. Balakrishna
Screenplay: G.D. Madgulkar **Lyrics**: Bharat Vyas
Music: Vasant Desai **Cast**: V. Shantaram, Sandhya,
Ulhas, B.M. Vyas, Baburao Pendharkar, Paul
Sharma, S.K. Singh, Keshavrao Date, G. Invagle,
Asha Devi.

A parable about human virtue, *Do Ankhen
Barah Haath* tells the story of a benevo-
lent police inspector Adinath (played by
Shantaram himself) who believes in the
innate decency of human beings. He
attempts to reform eight convicted crim-
inals through a holistic programme that
involves earning an honest livelihood by
tilling the land, but his efforts come up
against the narrow-mindedness of a rigid
society. The film was notable for its use
of expressionist imagery to indicate the
psychological states of the convicts.

Available Material:
NFAI: 1 release positive, 12 reels, in average condition. **Kiran Shantaram**: Original
camera negative; 1 dupe negative, 1
release positive; 15 reels each.

48 AJANTRIK

1957, Bengali | B&W, 120 minutes
Director: Ritwik Ghatak **Producer**: L.B. Films
Cinematographer: Dinen Gupta **Screenplay**: Ritwik
Ghatak **Music**: Ali Akbar Khan **Cast**: Kali Bannerjee,
Gangapada Basu, Anil Chatterjee, Tulsi Chakroborty,
Keshto Mukherjee, Kajal Gupta, Shriman Deepak,
Gyanesh Mukherjee, Satindra Bhattacharya, Jhurni,
Seeta Mukherjee.

Ajantrik was Ritwik Ghatak's first
released feature, based on a short narrative by the Bengali writer Subodh Gupta.
The film proposes "an emotional integra-
tion with the machine age" through the
story of an eccentric taxi-driver named
Bimal and his battered old Chevrolet,
whom he calls Jagaddal. The comical and
philosophical aspects of this strange relationship between man and machine are
explored as Bimal plies his trade in small-
town Bihar and the regions of the Oraon
tribe. Through their adventures, we realise that Jagaddal's days are numbered; the
jalopy breaks down irretrievably, and is
eventually dismantled to be sold as scrap.
A final scene suggests a continuation of
the cycle of life for this most animate of
inanimate objects.

Available Material: No original camera
negative survives. The film was originally
14 reels in length, but either the producer
or the director of the film edited out four
reels which depicted a sojourn among the
Oraon tribals. In 2006, NFDC submitted
a combined dupe negative of 10 reels to
the NFAI.
NFAI: 1 master positive, 10 reels, on
35 mm; 1 combined dupe negative, 10
reels, 1 combined dupe negative, 10
reels (NFDC), on 35 mm; 3 release positives, 10 reels, all on 35 mm, with a lot
of scratches.

Aparna Sen on *Ajantrik*

I saw Ritwik Ghatak's wonderful film
Ajantrik years ago, when I was barely in my
teens, but some of its images have remained
indelibly imprinted in my memory. For
instance, Kali Banerjee's expression when
a spanking new modern-age car crushes
his dented old dinner plate under its wheels
as he sits by the roadside, or his delight
when he receives a shining new plate in
place of the old one.

It is a tragedy that films such as *Ajantrik*
should fall victim to the ravages of time and
disappear forever from our archives. While
it is wonderful that most of Satyajit Ray's
films have been restored, restoration must
not be limited to the works of one filmmaker
only. We must try to enrich our archives by
restoring and preserving all those great
films that illuminate the cinematic history
of our country.

Buddhadeb Dasgupta on *Ajantrik*

Considering the time when *Ajantrik* was
made, it was the first attempt in the history of Indian cinema to go for a non-nar-
rative structure. Earlier, Ray had followed
a classical narrative pattern in *Pather
Panchali*, based purely on the work of the
book's author. From all aspects, *Ajantrik* is

Ajantrik

a path-breaking, uniquely creative film that still travels beyond time.

49 MADHUMATI

1958, Hindi | B&W, 179 minutes
Director: Bimal Roy **Producer**: Bimal Roy Productions **Cinematographer**: Dilip Gupta **Story**: Ritwik Ghatak **Dialogue**: Rajinder Singh Bedi **Lyrics**: Shailendra **Music**: Salil Chaudhury **Cast**: Dilip Kumar, Vyjayanthimala, Pran, Jayant, Johnny Walker, Tiwari, Mishra, Baij Sharma, Bhudo Advani, Jagdish, Sagar, Ranjeet Sud, Sheojibhai, Tarun Bose.

Madhumati was Bimal Roy's biggest commercial success, a rare genre film from a director known for his socialist approach to cinema. Here, Roy elevates a seemingly generic tale into something more enduring and elemental. All shadows and mist, the film tells the story of an engineer (Kumar) who takes shelter at an ancient mansion one night, only to be transported to a previous life when he worked for the lord of the mansion, and fell in love with the beautiful tribal maiden Madhumati. This romantic tale of reincarnation, ornamented with haunting songs from Salil Choudhury and atmospheric visuals from cinematographer Dilip Gupta, was influential in establishing a sub-genre of Hindi cinema. **Available Material:** In 2009, the NFAI printed 17 reels of the film from a dupe negative (ORWO stock). In 2010, the NFAI received from the Bimal Roy family the original camera negative and a dupe negative combined. Reel numbers 13, 14

and 15 of the original camera negative are not available and reels 2 and 11 are in a bad condition.

Vishal Bhardwaj on *Madhumati*

To see *Madhumati* restored and back on screen is a dream. Bimal Roy's magnificently captured reincarnation love story written by Ritwik Ghatak, Dilip Kumar's subtle performance in a melodrama and Salil Choudhury's haunting music stay with us even today.

Javed Akhtar on *Madhumati*

Madhumati was one of the finest romantic films. It had haunting music by Salil Chowdhury and the sensitivity with which Bimal Roy handled the actors brought out the best performances of Dilip Kumar and Vyjayanthimala. Bimal Roy had created a world of pure intensity and suspense, but the magic was in his romanticism. To me, it is a very precious film that must be preserved.

50 KAAGAZ KE PHOOL

1959, Hindi | B&W, 153 minutes
Director: Guru Dutt **Producer**: Guru Dutt Films **Cinematography**: V.K. Murthy **Screenplay**: Abrar Alvi **Lyrics**: Kaifi Azmi **Music**: S.D. Burman **Cast**: Guru Dutt, Waheeda Rehman, Johnny Walker, Mahesh Kaul, Veena Sapru, Baby Naaz, Minoo Mumtaz, Pratima Devi, Niloufer, Sulochana, Sheila Vaz, Bikram Kapoor.

Widely acclaimed today as a classic of world cinema, Guru Dutt's tale of a tormented director (Dutt) beaten down by his family, his muse, his audience and his fate, was not successful when it was first released. There are stretches in the film that appear morbidly prophetic today, as audiences violently reject the director's latest offering, to his devastation. However, V.K. Murthy's close-ups of Waheeda Rehman through the Cinemascope lens (this was the first Indian film to be shot in the Cinemascope format), the stunning chiaroscuro of the empty studio during '*Waqt ne kiya*', the sublime soundtrack by S.D. Burman and Kaifi Azmi and the lead performances by Rehman and Dutt, all remain eternally and gloriously romantic.

Available Material: India's first Cinemascope film was originally processed at the Famous Cine Lab, Tardeo. No original camera negative of this film survives. The NFAI has an original release positive of 8 double reels made from the original camera negative in 1959. This print, which has several scratches and vinegar syndrome, is the only surviving Cinemascope print of India's first Cinemascope film. In 2001, the NFAI made a combined dupe negative from this print of 16 reels.

NFAI: 1 original release positive, 8 double reels, scratches, vinegar syndrome; 1 combined dupe negative, 16 reels; 1 sound negative, 16 reels. **BFI**: 1 35 mm Academy format print from 1979, 16 reels without Cinemascope format, reel numbers 1, 4, 5 and 6 badly scratched, sound strangely missing for short segments.

Shyam Benegal on *Kaagaz ke Phool*

It is the very first Cinemascope film made in India, and one of the finest examples of the black-and-white photography of the times. The music score of the film was both unusual and well-orchestrated, with very fine lyrics written by Kaifi Azmi.

Before making this film, Guru Dutt had sent his cameraman V.K. Murthy to London to study under Oswald Morris how the Anamorphic lens worked and understand the challenges one would face in composing frames. I still remember watching this film on a rainy day in Maratha Mandir.

Kaagaz ke Phool

Amitabh Bachchan on *Kaagaz ke Phool*

Kaagaz ke Phool is my eternal favourite. I could spend a lifetime talking about this film—a film way ahead of its time. Beautifully photographed, with a great script, story and performance. . . what a film! That was pure genius. Every moment of the film is beautifully captured. Waheeda-*ji*'s incredibly aesthetic presence and Murthy *saheb*'s superb lighting created fantastic visuals. In the song 'Waqt ne kiya', the shot of Guru Dutt entering an empty studio lit by just one shaft of light is an unforgettable image. At the end of the film when he is running away and Waheeda-*ji* is chasing after him and the crowd surrounds her preventing her from following him, it is heart-wrenching. What a film! What a film!

51 SANGTYE AIKA

1959, Marathi | B&W, 157 minutes
Director: Anant Mane **Producer**: Chetana Chitra **Cinematographer**. I. Mohammed **Story**: C.C. Parki **Screenplay**: Vyankatesh Madgulkar **Lyrics**: G.D. Madgulkar **Music**: Vasant Pawar **Cast**: Sulochana, Hansa Wadkar, Jayashree Gadkar, Dada Salvi, Suryakant, Ratnamala, Neela, Pushpa Rane, Chandrakant, Vasant Shinde, Vasantrao Pahelwan, Kisanrao Agnihotri

A landmark film for its star Hansa Wadkar, *Sangtye Aika* is Marathi cinema's best-known Tamasha musical. This popular hit is an epic saga narrating a conflict over two generations between Mahadev Patil (Dada Salvi) and the dancer Chima (Wadkar). The film is known for its spectacularly staged bullock cart race, its realistic depiction of social hierarchy and exploitation in the Marathi hinterland, as well as its path-breaking use of the folk idioms of *lavani* and *tamasha* in performance to further the plot.

Available Material: The original camera negative does not survive. CBFC deposited 16 reels of the print in 1975 at NFAI. In 1995, the Directorate of Cultural Affairs, Mumbai deposited another 16 reels at the NFAI. Several 16 mm prints of this film are in existence thanks to its popularity resulting in it being shown in tent cinemas all over the state of Maharashtra.
NFAI: 1 Master positive, 16 reels; 1 release positive, 15 reels; 1 print, 16 reels (CBFC); 1 print, 16 reels (DCA)

52 GANGA JUMNA

1961, Hindi-Bhojpuri | Colour, 178 minutes
Director: Nitin Bose **Producer**: Dilip Kumar, Citizens Films **Cinematographer**: V. Babasaheb **Story, Screenplay**: Dilip Kumar **Dialogue**: Wajahat Mirza **Music**: Naushad **Lyrics**: Shakeel Badayuni **Cast**: Dilip Kumar, Vyjayanthimala, Nasir Khan, Azra, Kanhaiyalal, Leela Chitnis, Perveen Paul, Helen, Husn Bano, Ranjeet Sud, Khwaja Sabir Amar, Baby Naaz, Narbada Shankar

The first notable instance in Hindi cinema to use the trope of brothers placed on either side of the law by circumstance, *Gunga Jumna* was a hugely successful film which inspired several other landmark films like *Deewaar* and *Trishul*. The tyranny of the village landlord drives the rebellious Gunga (Dilip Kumar) to become a dacoit. His younger brother Jumna (Nasir Khan), meanwhile, is sent to the city to be educated and returns as a police officer. The stage is set for a powerful, and ultimately tragic, showdown between the brothers. The film was notable for its nuanced depiction of the Bhojpuri hinterland in terms of its attire, dialect, music and language.

Available Material: Originally shot in Technicolor and processed at Technicolor Ltd. in London through Ramnord Research Labs Pvt. Ltd., Mumbai, the original camera negative of 19 reels is at the Kay Laboratory in London. In 1972, an internegative made from the original camera negative was brought to the Bombay Film Laboratories Pvt. Ltd. to make more than a hundred prints for re-release. Later, in November 2009, the internegative was given to the NFAI. Kewal Suri, the present copyright-holder, has an internegative of 19 reels.

NFAI: Internegative of 19 reels picture; sound negative, 19 reels; 2 release positives, one of 9 double reels (complete film) and one of 16 reels. **Kewal Suri:** 1 internegative, 19 reels.

Vidhu Vinod Chopra on *Gunga Jumna*

Gunga Jumna had a very strong impact on me. I still remember how Dilip Kumar took my breath away. The Bhojpuri language that we have used in *PK* constantly reminded me of the great film. *Gunga Jumna* must be restored and preserved so that future generations can also partake of its brilliance.

Salim Khan on *Gunga Jumna*

When my son Salman saw the film for the first time, he could not believe Dilip Sahab's performance. He exclaimed, "I never imagined he was such a great actor! I have seen so many films over the years—Hindi films, foreign films, films of my contemporaries—I practically see one film a day! But I did not realise Dilip Sahab is such a great artist!" He was so mesmerised that he saw the film again the very next day!

I too had the same reaction to *Gunga Jumna*. In fact when I saw it I thought of giving up acting! I watched the film five times and thought, what's the point of pursuing acting, I will never be able to match this performance!

Amitabh Bachchan on *Gunga Jumna*

The 1961 *Gunga Jumna* of Nitin Bose—another great film, another great story. This film has inspired many other versions of films about two brothers, one of them being on the wrong side of the law and the ensuing conflict between them. There are many reflections of them in my own films too, like *Deewar*. The lavish produc-

tion of this film was set in Avadh. I myself spoke Avadhi for 15 years before staying in Bombay. When I saw the performance of Dilip *saheb*, I couldn't believe that a person living in Bombay could speak Avadhi so authentically.

Mother India, *Gunga Jumna*, all are great films. I hope they can be restored and kept for eternity. They need to be preserved.

53 KOMAL GANDHAR

1961, Bengali | B & W, 134 minutes
Director: Ritwik Ghatak **Producer**: Chitrakalpa
Cinematography: Dilip Ranjan Mukhopadhyay
Screenplay: Ritwik Ghatak **Music**: Jyotirindra Moitra
Cast: Supriya Choudhury, Abanish Banerjee, Abhi Bhattacharya, Chitra Mandal, Bijon Bhattacharya, Mani Srimani, Satyabrata Chattopadhyay, Satindra Bhattacharya, Gyanesh Mukherjee

Set in the world of radical theatre in 50s Bengal, Ghatak's film caused a major controversy in its time. The narrative probes the effects of the Partition of Bengal (an abiding preoccupation in Ghatak's life and work) as it depicts rivalry and factionalism in a theatre group putting a production of *Shakuntala*. Two of the members discover they are both refugees from East Bengal, steeped in pain and longing for their lost homeland, and become lovers.

Sangtye Aika

Mudiyanaya Puthran

സുപ്രസിദ്ധമായൊരു നാടകകഥ ചലച്ചിത്രത്തിൽ

ചന്ദ്രതാരാ പ്രൊഡക്ഷൻസ്

മുടിയനായപുത്രൻ

CHANDRATARA നിർമ്മാണം ടി.കെ. പരീക്കുട്ടി സംവിധാനം രാമുകാര്യാട്ട് ഛായാഗ്രഹണം വിൻസൻറ്

At several instances in the film, there is an attempt to make sense of this loss, as in the famous tracking shot along abandoned railway tracks running up to the Indian bank of the Padma river, which is followed by an abrupt blackout, conveying the brutal, irrational ruptures of Partition.

Available Material: The original camera negative does not survive. CBFC, Kolkata deposited a print of 10 reels at the NFAI. **NFAI:** 1 combined dupe negative of 14 reels; 2 release positives, one of 14 reels and one of 10 reels, both on 35 mm; 1 sound negative, 7 reels on both sides; 1 print, 10 reels (CBFC)

54 SAPTAPADI

1961, Bengali | B&W, 163 minutes
Director: Ajoy Kar **Producer**: Aalochhaya Productions **Cinematographer**: Ajoy Kar **Story**: Tarashankar Bandopadhyay **Screenplay**: Ajoy Kar **Lyrics**: Gauri Prasanna Majumdar **Music**: Hemanta Kumar Mukhopadhyay **Cast**: Uttam Kumar, Suchitra Sen, Chhabi Biswas, Chhaya Debi.

Based on a Tarashankar Bandopadhyay novel, the film is set in the years before the independence of India. Fellow medical students Krishnendu (Kumar) and Rita (Sen) fall in love with each other but face opposition because she is Christian and he is Hindu. Rebelling against his strict, conservative father (Biswas), Krishnendu

goes into exile, while Rita becomes an alcoholic, and later joins the army. Years later, they are reunited in the midst of World War II. Featuring an immensely popular soundtrack by Hemanta Kumar, this is one of the finest films from the golden pair of Bengali cinema, Uttam Kumar and Suchitra Sen.

Available Material: No original camera negative or dupe negative remains. **NFAI:** 1 release positive, 17 reels.

55 MUDIYANAYA PUTHRAN

1961, Malayalam | B&W, 147 minutes
Director: Ramu Kariat **Producer**: Chandrathara Productions **Cinematographer**: A. Vincent **Screenplay**: Thoppil Bhasi **Lyrics**: P. Bhaskaran **Music**: Baburaj **Cast**: Sathyan, P.J. Anthony, Adoor Bhasi,Ambika, Kumari, Kambiserri, Kottayam, Chellappan, P.A. Thomas.

The wastrel Rajan (Sathyan) loses his girl (Ambika) to his elder brother Gopal and is eventually thrown out of the parental home by his mother. Through a series of events, the two brothers find themselves on opposing sides in a showdown between workers and management: Rajan leading the workers, while the management of the company is represented by Gopal, who additionally suspects the relationship between his wife and brother. This political melodrama (a unique genre of the Malayalam cinema) was actively supported by the Kerala branch of the Communist Party of India (CPI) and was particularly noted for capturing the spirit of the times.

Available Material:
NFAI: 1 release positive, 15 reels.

56 SAHIB BIWI AUR GHULAM

1962, Hindi | B&W, 152 minutes
Director: Abrar Alvi **Producer**: Guru Dutt Films **Cinematographer**: V.K. Murthy **Story**: Based on Bimal Mitra's novel *Sahib Biwi Golam* **Screenplay**: Abrar Alvi **Lyrics**: Shakeel Badayuni **Music**: Hemanta Kumar Mukhopadhyay **Cast**: Mala Sinha, Guru Dutt, Rehman, Waheeda Rehman, Nasir Hussain, Sapru, Sajjan, S.N. Banerjee, Dhumal,

Krishna, Dhawan, Jawahar Kaul, Harindranath Chattopadhyay, Minoo Mumtaz, Pratima Devi, Ranjit Kumari, Bikram Kapoor.

Based on a classic novel, *Sahib Biwi aur Ghulam* is a tragic ode to the *zamindari* culture of 19th century Bengal, as well as a scathing critique of its decadence. The story is seen through the eyes of the shy, halting Bhootnath (Dutt), who arrives at the Choudhury mansion in search of work. He is drawn into the lives of its inhabitants, especially the beautiful lonely Chhoti Bahu (Kumari), who has been cast aside by her alcoholic husband Chhote Sarkar (Rehman) who prefers the company of dancing girls. The film featured the brilliant cinematography of V.K. Murthy and a richly evocative soundtrack by Hemanta Kumar and Shakeel Badayuni.

Available Material: Shot on safety base and originally processed at the Famous Cine Lab, Tardeo. No original camera negative or dupe negative or master positive of the film survives. The only complete material of the film is with the NFAI. The Guru Dutt family deposited 11 reels of the sound negative at the NFAI. The NFAI made the other 5 reels of the sound negative.

NFAI: Sound negative; 3 release positives, 16 reels each, all on 35 mm.

Kundan Shah on *Sahib Biwi aur Ghulam*

I have seen *Sahib Biwi aur Ghulam* more than a hundred times and continue viewing it every month to inspire myself. A complex theme embellished with the extraordinary tapestry of cinema. A classic forever!

Shyam Benegal on *Sahib Biwi aur Ghulam*

By far the most accomplished of all the films to emerge from the Guru Dutt banner was *Sahib Biwi aur Ghulam* which, ironically, was directed by his writer Abrar Alvi.

---

57 SUBARNAREKHA

1962, Bengali | B&W, 143 minutes
Director: Ritwik Ghatak **Producer:** J.J. Films
Cinematographer: Dilip Ranjan Mukhopadhyay
Story: Radheshyam Jhunjhunwala **Music:** Bahadur Khan **Cast:** Madhabi Mukherjee, Abhi Bhattacharya, Bijon Bhattacharya, Satindra Bhattacharya, Geeta De, Sriman Tarun, Abanish Banerjee, Jahar Roy.

Subarnarekha

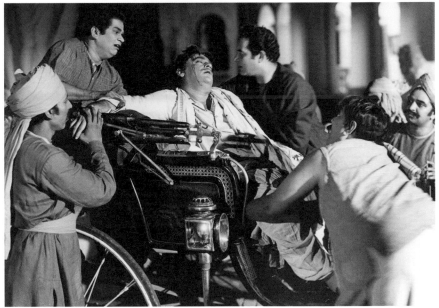

Sahib Biwi aur Ghulam

Ghatak's complex film tells the story of Ishwar Chakroborty (A. Bhattacharya), a refugee from East Bengal, and his little sister Seeta, who start out in a camp after Partition. Ishwar adopts the child of an Untouchable woman and brings him up as his own child along with Seeta. In their youth, however, Seeta (M. Mukherjee) and the adopted child Abhiram (S. Bhattacharya) fall in love with each other, leading to several tragic turns in the story. Ghatak brings a tragic sense of the disruption caused by Partition to the film's sequences, at times taking recourse to the codes of melodrama abruptly. The

film abounds with literary and cinematic quotations, besides deploying Ghatak's unconventional approach to music and sound design.

Available Material: NFAI: 2 dupe negatives, 15 reels each, both 35 mm; 1 sound negative, 15 reels; 4 release positives, 15 reels each; two 16 mm release positives, 3 reels each.

Madhabi Mukherjee on *Subarnarekha*

Subarnarekha is an important film that needs to be restored, so that future generations understand that such a unique kind of film existed. *Subarnarekha* was both modern and historically rooted and you can easily see the context in this film. Ghatak's style of heightened melodrama was different from Satyajit Ray's style of realism, and it is important for future filmmakers to understand these different styles of filmmaking.

I still remember the scene where Ghatak took a close-up of my eyes. Instead of using a regular camera lens, he used a spectacle lens of + 7 power held in front of the camera to get an enhanced distorted feel.

58 CHEMMEEN

1965, Malayalam | Colour, 140 minutes
Director: Ramu Kariat **Producer**: Babu Ismail Sait, Kanmani Films **Cinematographers**: Marcus Bartley, U. Rajagopal **Story**: Based on Thakazhy Shivshankar Pillai's novel *Chemmeen*. **Dialogue**: S.L. Puram Sadanandan **Lyrics**: Vyalar Rama Varma **Music**: Salil Chaudhury **Cast**: Sheela, Madhu, Kottarakara Sreedharan Nair, Sathyan, S.P. Pillai, Adoor Bhawani, Adoor Pakanjam, Lata, Kottayam Chellappan, Rajakumari, J.A.R. Anand, Paravoor Bharathan, Kothamangalam Ali, Philomena.

Based on a widely acclaimed bestseller, *Chemmeen* portrays the lives of fisherfolk in Kerala with great detail and an almost fable-like romanticism. The story draws from the prevalent myth in coastal Kerala that if a fisherwoman has been unfaithful to her husband in his absence, Kadalamma, the sea goddess will consume him. One of the earliest colour films in Malayalam, it had spectacular photography by Marcus Bartley which won the film a gold medal for cinematography at the Cannes Film Festival, besides inspiring generations of cinematographers since. It was the first south Indian film to win the National Award for Best Feature Film.

Available Material: No original camera negative or internegative of the film remains.
Chalachitra Academy Archive, Thiruvananthapuram: 35 mm print, 7 double reels.
NFAI: 1 release positive, 14 reels.

Santosh Sivan on *Chemmeen*

Chemmeen was one of the first films in colour. An adaptation of a literary work, it caressed the life of the fishermen folk. The film drew me into the midst of their lives,

and it also made the sea a character. It is a film that I see often, and it has a timeless quality.

59 GUIDE

1965, Hindi | Colour, 183 minutes
Director: Vijay Anand **Producer**: Navketan Film **Cinematography**: Fali Mlstry **Story**: Based on R.K. Narayan's novel *The Guide* **Screenplay**: Vijay Anand **Lyrics**: Shailendra **Music**: S.D. Burman **Cast**: Dev Anand, Waheeda Rehman, Leela Chitnis, Kishore Shahu, Gajanan Jagirdar, Anwar Hussain, Ulhas, Rashid Khan

Adapted from a classic novel, *Guide* was made in Hindi and English versions, the latter co-scripted by author Pearl S. Buck. An intimate epic, the film portrays the relationship between Rosie (Rehman) a dancer who is seduced away from her claustrophobic marriage with Marco (Sahu), her archaeologist husband, by the tourist guide (Raju) who helps her pursue her dream of becoming a successful dancer. Despite the theme of the film (unconventional for commercial Hindi cinema), *Guide* was an enormous hit when released, aided in no small measure by a soundtrack for the ages by S.D. Burman and Shailendra, featuring such gems as *'Gaata rahe mera dil'*, *'Tere mere sapne'*, *'Piya tose naina laage re'* and *'Aaj phir jeene ki tamanna hai'*.

Available Material: The film was originally processed at Pathe Lab Inc., New York. **Navketan Films:** Original camera nega-

Chemmeen

tive, not in a great condition; internegative of 11 double reels each; sound negative of 11 double reels. **NFAI:** 2 release
positives, 11 double reels each; all on 35
mm, in which colour has faded.

Olavum Theeravum

Waheeda Rehman on *Guide*

I wasn't sure at first that I wanted to
do *Guide*. But Dev Anand and Vijay Anand
insisted that I play Rosie. Dev *saheb* told me
he could not consider anyone else in the
role, so I agreed. I felt close to the character
of Rosie, because she is a person who wants
to find a graceful way of determining her
own fate. It is a film that was bold in theme
while being executed beautifully. It was a
very important film for me personally, and
now I can see that it is an equally important
film in the history of Hindi cinema.

60 OLAVUM THEERAVUM

1969, Malayalam | B&W, 120 minutes
Director: P.N. Menon **Producer**: P.A. Backer
Cinematography: Ravi Varma **Screenplay**: M.T.
Vasudevan Nair **Lyrics**: P. Bhaskaran **Music**:
Baburaj **Cast**: Madhu, Nellikode Bhaskaran,
Usha Nandini, Philomina, Jose Prakash, Paravoor
Bharathan, Kunjava, Mala, Nilambur Aisha,
Nilambur Balan.

With its extensive use of local accents and
outdoor locations, *Olavum Theeravum*
marked the beginning of a realistic art-
house aesthetic for Malayalam cinema.
The plot is centred on the story of the
Muslim timber trader Bapputty (Madhu)
whose only love Nabeesa (Usha Nandini)
is married off by her money-grabbing
mother to a rich trader Kunjali (Prakash).
It ends in tragedy, with Bapputty unable
to save Nabeesa from committing suicide.
The film's emphasis on realism (famed
author M. T. Vasudevan Nair wrote the
script) was highly influential for a whole
generation of Malayalam filmmakers.

Available Material: No original camera
negative or dupe negative survives.
**Chalachitra Academy Archive, Thiruvan-
anthapuram:** 35 mm print, 13 reels. **NFAI:**
1 release positive, 13 reels.

M.T. Vasudevan Nair on *Olavum Theeravum*

For me, it's *Olavum Theeravum* by P. N.
Menon. It was a trend setter: the camera
was taken out from the studio sets to
authentic locations for the first time.

We would like to thank P.K. Nair, founder of the NFAI and advisor to the Foundation for helping us compile this list. This task would not have been possible without the cooperation of the NFAI, especially the Director, Alpana Pant Sharma, K.A. Dhiwar, the Film Preservation Officer and the film librarian, N.S. Alhat, who helped us with the research and inventory of material. We would also like to thank Kiran Shantaram; Hosi Wadia at Bombay Film Laboratories Pvt. Ltd.; Rajkumar Seksaria at the Famous Cine Lab, Tardeo; Mamaji at R.K. Films; R. Gowri Kumar at AVM Film Studios; Mohan Krishnan at the Prasad Group; Gopi Krishna at Chalachitra Academy, Kerala; Shaukat Khan at Mehboob Studios Pvt. Ltd.; Mehelli Modi; Karan Bali; Pinaki Chakraborty at New Theatre Films; Kieron Webb at the British Film Institute; Céline Ruivo at Cinémathèque Française; Paolo Cherchi Usai, Jared Case and Daniela Currò at George Eastman House; Briana Cechova at the National Film Archive of the Czech Republic; and Peter Bagrov at Gosfilmofond.
Film synopses compiled by Bishaldeb Halder. Film credits and details sourced from *The Encyclopaedia of Indian Cinema* by Ashish Rajadhyaksha and Paul Willemen with permission.

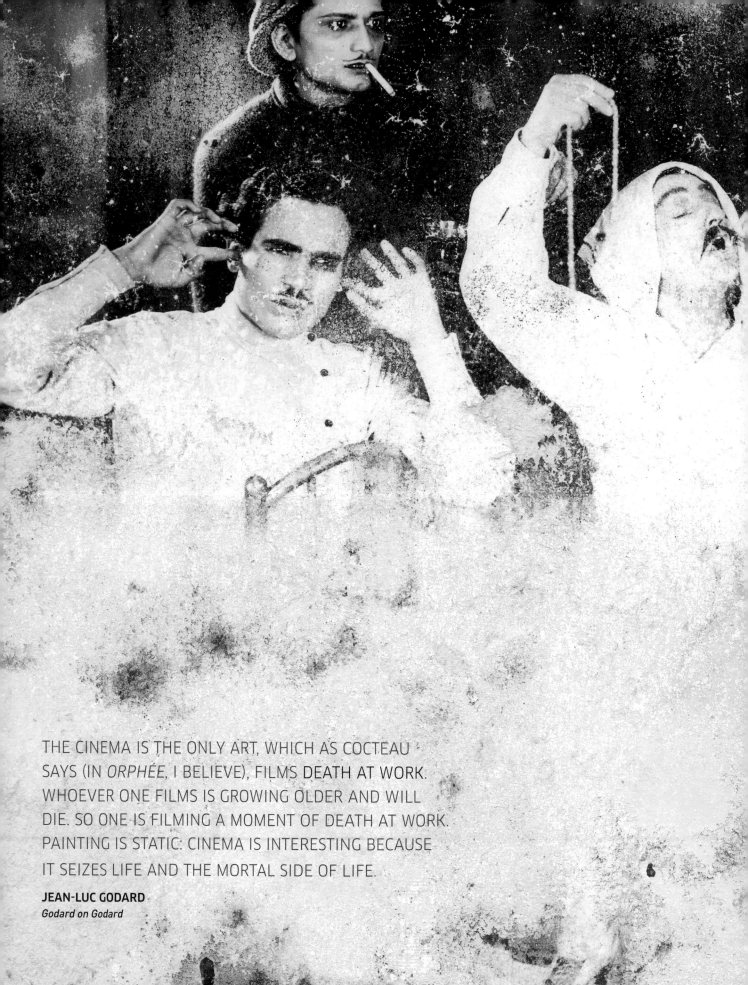

THE CINEMA IS THE ONLY ART, WHICH AS COCTEAU
SAYS (IN *ORPHÉE*, I BELIEVE), FILMS **DEATH AT WORK.**
WHOEVER ONE FILMS IS GROWING OLDER AND WILL
DIE. SO ONE IS FILMING A MOMENT OF DEATH AT WORK.
PAINTING IS STATIC: CINEMA IS INTERESTING BECAUSE
IT SEIZES LIFE AND THE MORTAL SIDE OF LIFE.

JEAN-LUC GODARD
Godard on Godard